OREMUS

"This book represents an inspiring continuation of the Second Vatican Council's desire to form the faithful through a deeper appreciation of the Latin language. In a way both beautiful and accessible, *Oremus* provides a wealth of Catholic prayers for the People of God. It is a valuable addition to any home library and a wonderful aid for those who wish to familiarize themselves with the Church's premier language of prayer and worship."

Fr. Blake Britton
Priest of the Diocese of Orlando
Word on Fire blog contributor

"Few things bring me that feeling of connection with our Catholic tradition like lifting up my heart to our Lord in Latin, and with *Oremus* I'm finally confident enough to do it with consistency. This collection of prayers, in both Latin and English, has brought me closer to our Lord and his Church, and it will surely do likewise for everyone who adds it to their collection."

Tommy Tighe
Author of *The Catholic Hipster Handbook*

"In a materialist world that caters to every whim and trendy fashion, there is a longing in our hearts for the ancient and the transcendent. Praying in Latin connects the reader to Christians throughout the ages who have prayed the very same beautiful words no matter when or where they lived. This treasury makes Latin prayers accessible to the modern English-speaking reader."

Haley Stewart
Catholic podcaster, blogger, and author of *The Grace of Enough*

"This little treasury of Latin prayers is inviting and easy to use. It offers a beautiful selection from across the ages, and ranges from the very short and easy to memorize to longer prayers, litanies, and psalms. It is a joy to see this appear in print."

John Cavadini
Director of the McGrath Institute for Church Life
University of Notre Dame

OREMUS

A TREASURY OF LATIN PRAYERS

WITH ENGLISH TRANSLATIONS

AVE MARIA PRESS AVE Notre Dame, Indiana

Latin Psalm texts are from the Sixto-Clementine Vulgate.

English translations of Psalms are from the translation by Ronald Knox, *The Holy Bible: A Translation from the Latin Vulgate in the Light of the Hebrew and Greek Originals* © 1950, 2012 Archdiocese of Westminster, published by Burns & Oates, London, England.

Translations of Latin prayers provided by Christopher Bailey.

———————————————————

© 2020 Ave Maria Press, Inc.

Founded in 1865, Ave Maria Press is a ministry of the United States Province of Holy Cross.

www.avemariapress.com

Paperback: ISBN-13 978-1-59471-989-9

E-book: ISBN-13 978-1-59471-990-5

Cover image © gettyimages.com.

Cover and text design by Brian C. Conley.

Printed and bound in the United States of America.

Library of Congress Cataloging-in-Publication Data
Names: Bailey, Christopher, 1964- translator.
Title: Oremus : a treasury of Latin prayers with English translations / translated by Christopher Bailey.
Other titles: Oremus. English.
Description: Notre Dame, Indiana : Ave Maria Press, 2020. | English translation side by side with original Latin. | Summary: "Oremus offers traditional Latin prayers and literal English translations presented in a side-by-side format"—Provided by publisher.
Identifiers: LCCN 2020015817 (print) | LCCN 2020015818 (ebook) | ISBN 9781594719899 (paperback) | ISBN 9781594719905 (ebook)
Subjects: LCSH: Catholic Church--Prayers and devotions. | Prayers.
Classification: LCC BX2149.2 .O74 2020 (print) | LCC BX2149.2 (ebook) | DDC 242/.802--dc23
LC record available at https://lccn.loc.gov/2020015817
LC ebook record available at https://lccn.loc.gov/2020015818

CONTENTS

Publisher's Note on Scripture Versions and Translations

It may surprise readers that while numerous translations of the Bible are approved, there is no "official" Catholic translation. The Latin text of the Psalms included in this book is taken from the Sixto-Clementine edition of the Vulgate (1592, 1593, 1598), which includes St. Jerome's second and most popular version of the Book of Psalms known as the "Gallican Psalter." This psalter was at the center of the historical tradition of worship in the Church over many centuries. The English translation of the Psalms provided here is from the Church-approved Knox translation (1949). Knox is the most recent English translation of the Vulgate, and is considered a more readable alternative to the Douay-Rheims. It is not currently used in any form of Catholic liturgy.

Interestingly, there is a more recent edition of the Latin Vulgate known as the *Nova Vulgata*. This edition was originally commissioned by Pope Pius X in 1907. The work of translation stretched across several decades, and the complete text was ultimately promulgated under Pope John Paul II in 1979. The *Nova Vulgata* has been designated the "typical" Latin biblical text of the Catholic Church and is used in the contemporary Roman rite.

One cannot entirely avoid scholarly and ecclesial debate when selecting biblical texts and translations. Each version has value, and each invariably has strengths and weaknesses. It is our hope that every available translation can be appreciated for what it is, and that the editorial choices made for this publication are not interpreted as belonging to, or promoting, any particular perspective.

INTRODUCTION

God hears our prayers in every language and in none; he hears our wordless cries of joy or pain, and he also hears our silence. In a certain sense, then, we need not worry about how to pray. And yet, the request that Jesus' first disciples made on the shores of the Sea of Galilee two millennia ago is one we still make today: "Lord, teach us to pray" (Lk 11:1).

Why pray in Latin? If you're holding this book, it is likely that you have your own answer to that question. It might be curiosity or nostalgia, perhaps a desire for something new or something very, very old that drew you to *Oremus*. But whether the Latin language is already part of your spiritual life or not, you likely have felt a desire—maybe even a calling—to strengthen and express the connection between your Christian faith and the faith of the Church across the ages.

You are not alone! Today, there is a growing number of Catholics who are interested in the rich tradition of Latin prayer. Many are looking for ways to integrate at least some of that tradition into their personal prayer and devotional practices. Some, of all ages and backgrounds, have found a spiritual home in parishes that offer the Traditional Latin Mass. Others simply appreciate the beauty and depth of our more ancient prayers and practices. More and more, we share a desire both to experience and to express the transcendence of sacred mystery. Latin is the spiritual inheritance of every Catholic.

There are plenty of good reasons for praying in Latin, reasons that reach all the way back to the first centuries of our faith. After all, Latin has been the language of the Catholic Church in the West for eighteen hundred years, and it is still the Church's official language. All Church documents and liturgical texts are written in Latin. While the Mass is now offered in the vernacular, that is a relatively recent historical development. English, Portuguese, Vietnamese, Tagalog, and all other versions of our liturgy are translations from the official Latin original. Because Latin is *the* language of the Church in the West, most of our traditional prayers and devotions were also originally written—and prayed—in Latin. In other words, most of what today's Catholics pray is prayed *in translation*.

The prayers in this book are prayers Catholics have loved for generations and, in many cases, for centuries. They were composed in Latin, and in the original Latin they have a beauty that no translation can quite capture. Many of them are poetry, in which the sounds and rhythm of the words are as important as their meaning. To pray them in Latin is to experience them the way the original composers intended.

When you pray in Latin, you are tangibly connecting yourself with an ancient tradition that goes back eighteen centuries. You are speaking the language of the Roman martyrs, theologians such as St. Jerome and St. Augustine, later scholars such as St. Bonaventure and St. Thomas Aquinas, and a countless host of faithful who have gone before you.

You are using the very same words as all those generations who still live in Christ and pray with us as the Communion of Saints.

Latin is also a universal language, one that no one in our times can claim as his "native tongue." Wherever you are in the world, someone is praying in Latin. When you pray in Latin, you are joining the prayers of Catholics in every corner of the earth. They may live in places you would have to look up in an atlas, but you are speaking the same language. The barriers of speech and culture that would ordinarily separate you have disappeared. When you pray in Latin, you are making the unity of the Church more visible.

Praying in Latin also gives us a way of separating our everyday speech from the words we use to speak to God. You will probably never write an email or shout at another driver in Latin. So Latin gives you a special way of speaking that is reserved for God, the angels, and the saints. While Latin was the vernacular for ancient believers, for us it can be language that is set apart for prayer and prayer alone.

Of course, it is also important to know what you are praying. The English translations provided on the left pages of *Oremus* are meant to be guides to understanding the Latin prayers on the right. They follow the Latin a little more closely than many of the traditional and official English versions of these prayers. But at the same time, they need to be good English, so they don't follow the Latin word for word. In general, the English translation preserves the Latin word order where it could be done without torturing the English; otherwise, the translation follows natural English word order.

Learning to pray in Latin isn't the same as learning the Latin language. Even those who have not previously studied Latin can learn Latin prayers. This book has the tools you need to do so. It's best to begin with the pronunication guide that follows. *Oremus!*

Pronunciation Guide

Pronouncing Ecclesiastical Latin

Learning to pronounce Latin is easy, because you can almost always tell from the spelling how a word is pronounced.

If you learned Latin at school, you might have learned "classical Latin" pronunciation, which is our best guess at how Latin was pronounced at about the time of Julius Caesar. Catholics traditionally use a later pronunciation of Latin, which is a little more like Italian. We call it "ecclesiastical Latin."

Vowels

Vowels in Latin are pronounced the way they are in most European languages. Each vowel has a long and a short sound.

A: Long sounds like A in *father*; short sounds like A in *about*.

E: Long sounds like E in *they*; short sounds like E in *pet*.

I: Long sounds like I in *machine*; short sounds like I in *fit*.

O: Long sounds like O in *hope*; short sounds like O in *oppress*.

U: Long sounds like U in *flute*; short sounds like U in *put*.

It is not always obvious from the spelling whether a vowel is long or short. If you give every accented vowel its full long value, however, you will be close to correct and easily understood.

There are also diphthongs—combinations of two vowels that make one sound.

AE and OE sound like AY in *day*. In this book, we have chosen to render them as *ae* and *oe* rather than *æ* and *œ*.

AU sounds like OU in *loud*.

EU has no equivalent in English: make the sound by beginning with E as in *let* and then sliding into U as in *rule*. In this book, you will find the diphthong EU only in the word *Eucharístiae*.

If they do not form a diphthong, all the vowels are pronounced separately: *fílii* is pronounced *FEE-lee-ee*.

(The rare diphthongs EI and UI do not occur in this book. The vowels here will always be pronounced separately, so *Dei* is pronounced *DAY-ee,* and *fuit* is pronounced *FOO-it.*)

CONSONANTS

All the consonants are pronounced as they are in English, with these exceptions.

C sounds like C in *cat* most of the time. But, as in English, it softens before E and I, and before the diphthongs AE and OE, which sound like E. A soft C in ecclesiastical Latin sounds like our *ch* in *church*, the way it does in Italian, so *pacem* sounds like *PAH-chem.*

CC, when it comes before E, I, AE, OE, or Y, sound like our *tch* in *watch*, so *ecce* sounds like *ETCH-ay*

SC in front of E, I, AE, or OE softens the consonant more so that it sounds like English SH, so *renáscimur* sounds like *reh-NASH-i-moor.*

CH sounds like our CH in *architect,* not our CH in *church.*

G sounds like G in *got* most of the time, but before E and I (and AE and OE) it sounds like English G in *gentle.*

The combination GN sounds like NY in *canyon.* So *agnus* is pronounced *AN-yus.*

H is silent, except in the words *mihi* and *nihil,* where it sounds like K.

PH sounds like PH in *philosophy.*

S is pronounced like S most of the time, but a single S between vowels is pronounced like an English Z. (We often do the same thing in English, as in *nasal.*) So *sit* is pronounced *sit,* and *essent* is pronounced *ES-sent,* bur *rosa* is pronounced *RO-za.*

T is pronounced like our T most of the time, but before I and another vowel it sounds like TS. So *laudátio* sounds like *lou-DAH-tsee-o.*

TH is pronounced like T.

X sounds like KS most of the time. But when the prefix *ex-* is followed by a vowel, X sounds like GZ. So *rex* sounds like *reks,* and *extrémae* sounds like *eks-TRAY-may,* but *exíre* sounds like *egz-EE-reh*.

Z (which is rare in Latin) sounds like DZ.

A NOTE ABOUT THE LETTER J

Ancient Latin alphabets did not have a letter J. Instead, the letter I was sometimes used as a consonant. It is pronounced like our consonant Y, so that *Iesu* is pronounced *YAY-zu*. As time passed, some Church texts began to use the letter J; others still do not. In this book, as in most editions of the Pio-Clementine Vulgate Bible, the letter J is not used. The words *Iesu, iubiláte, and cuius* are examples of those which some publications render *Jesu, jubiláte,* and *cujus.*

ACCENT

There are relatively simple rules that determine on which syllable the accent falls in a Latin word, but they involve knowing which vowels are long and short. In many Latin prayer books, including this one, the accents are marked in words of more than two syllables. (If the accent falls on a diphthong, it is written over the second letter of the diphthong, as in *saécula.*) In words of two syllables, the accent is *always* on the first syllable. The umlaut used in names like *Michaël* indicates that the vowel is to be pronounced as a separate syllable.

MORNING PRAYERS

Sign of the Cross

In the name of the Father, and of the
Son, and of the Holy Spirit. Amen.

Invitatory

Lord, open up my lips,
And my mouth will proclaim your praise.
God, reach out to my assistance.
Lord, hasten to my support.
Glory to the Father, and to the Son, and to the Holy Spirit,
as it was in the beginning, and now, and always, and into the
   ages of ages.
Amen. (Alleluia.)

Morning Offering

Lord Jesus Christ, in union with that divine intention by
which on earth, through your most sacred Heart, you offered praises to God, and are offering them now in the Sacrament of the Eucharist everywhere in the world, up to the
completion of the age: I, throughout this entire day, in imi-
tation of the most sacred Heart of blessed Mary ever Virgin
immaculate, most willingly offer you all my intentions and
thoughts, all my affections and desires, all my works and
words. Amen.

Signum Crucis

In nómine Patris, et Fílii, et Spíritus
Sancti. Amen.

Lauds

Dómine, lábia mea apéries,
Et os meum annunciábit laudem tuam.
Deus, in adiutórium meum inténde.
Dómine, ad adiuvándum me festína.
Glória Patri, et Fílio, et Spíritui sancto,
sicut erat in princípio, et nunc, et semper, et in saécula
    saeculórum.
Amen. (Allelúia.)

Dómine Iesu Christe, In Unióne

Dómine Iesu Christe, in unióne illíus divínae intentiónis,
qua in terris, per sanctíssimum Cor tuum, laudes Deo
persolvísti, et nunc in Eucharístiae Sacraménto úbique
terrárum persólvis, usque ad consummatiónem saéculi:
ego, per hanc diem íntegram, ad imitatiónem sanctíssimi
Cordis beátae Maríae semper Vírginis immaculátae, tibi
libentíssime óffero omnes meos intentiónes et cogitatiónes,
omnes meos afféctus et desidéria, ómnia mea ópera et verba.
Amen.

Canticle of Zechariah

Blessed be the Lord God of Israel,
because he has visited and made redemption for his people
and has set up a horn of salvation for us
in the house of David his servant.
As it was spoken through the mouth of his holy ones,
who were of old, his prophets:
salvation from our enemies,
and from the hand of all who hate us:
For showing mercy to our fathers,
and to remember his holy testament:
the oath that he swore to Abraham our father,
that he was going to give us;
so that without fear, freed from the hand of our enemies,
we should serve him
in holiness and justice in his presence
for all our days.
And you, child, will be called a prophet of the Most High:
for you will go before the face of the Lord to prepare his ways:
to give knowledge of salvation to his people
for the remission of their sins
through the heart of mercy of our God,
in which he will visit us, the dawn from on high:
to give light to those who are sitting in the darkness and
    shadow of death,
to direct our feet into the way of peace.

BENEDÍCTUS

Benedíctus Dóminus Deus Ísrael,
quia visitávit et fecit redemptiónem plebis suae
Et eréxit cornu salútis nobis
in domo David púeri sui.
Sicut locútus est per os sanctórum,
qui a saéculo sunt, prophetárum eius:
Salútem ex inímicis nostris,
et de manu ómnium qui óderunt nos:
Ad faciéndam misericórdiam cum pátribus nostris:
et memorári testaménti sui sancti:
Jusiurándum quod jurávit ad Ábraham patrem nostrum,
datúrum se nobis;
Ut sine timóre, de manu inimicórum nostrórum liberáti,
serviámus illi
in sanctitáte et iustítia coram ipso
ómnibus diébus nostris.
Et tu puer, prophéta Altíssimi vocáberis:
praeíbis enim ante fáciem Dómini paráre vias eius:
Ad dandam sciéntiam salútis plebi eius
in remissiónem peccatórum eórum
Per víscera misericórdiae Dei nostri,
in quibus visitábit nos, óriens ex alto:
Illumináre his qui in tenébris et in umbra mortis sedent,
ad dirigéndos pedes nostros in viam pacis.

PRAYERS AT MEALS

Before a Meal

Bless, Lord, us and these your gifts, which from your generosity we are about to receive. Through Christ our Lord. Amen.

After a Meal

We give you thanks, omnipotent God, for all of your benefits, you who live and reign into the ages of ages. Amen.

V. May God give us his peace.

R. And eternal life.

Amen.

BÉNEDIC, DÓMINE

Bénedic, Dómine, nos et haec tua dona, quae de tua largitáte sumus sumptúri. Per Christum Dóminum nostrum. Amen.

ÁGIMUS TIBI GRÁTIAS

Ágimus tibi grátias, omnípotens Deus, pro univérsis benefíciis tuis, qui vivis et regnas in saécula saeculórum. Amen.

V. Deus det nobis suam pacem.

R. *Et vitam aetérnam.*

Amen.

Evening Prayers

Canticle of Mary

My soul glorifies the Lord,
and my spirit has rejoiced in God my savior,
because he has paid attention to the humility of his handmaid.
For behold, from now on all generations will call me blessed,
because he who is mighty has done great things for me, and
holy is his name,
and his mercy belongs to those who fear him, from generation to generation.
He has shown might in his arm; he has scattered the proud
in the thoughts of their hearts.
He has thrust the powerful from their seats and exalted the
humble.
The hungry he has filled with good things, and the rich he
has sent away empty.
He has raised up Israel his servant, remembering his mercy,
as he spoke to our fathers, to Abraham and his seed forever.
Amen.

Canticle of Simeon

Now you are sending away your servant, Lord, according to
your word, in peace:
because my eyes have seen your salvation
which you have prepared before the face of all the peoples:
a light for the revelation of the nations, and the glory of your
people Israel. Amen.

Magníficat

Magníficat ánima mea Dóminum,
Et exultávit spíritus meus in Deo salutári meo,
Quia respéxit humilitátem ancíllae suae.
Ecce enim ex hoc beátam me dicent omnes generatiónes,
Quia fécit mihi mágna qui pótens est, et sánctum nómen eius.

Et misericórdia eius in progénies et progénies timéntibus
    eum.
Fécit poténtiam in bráchio suo; dispérsit supérbos mente
    cordis sui.
Depósuit poténtes de sede et exaltávit húmiles.

Esuriéntes implévit bonis, et dívites dimísit inánes.

Suscépit Ísrael púerum suum, recordátus misericórdiae suae,
Sicut locútus est ad patres nostros, Ábraham, et sémini eius
    in saécula.
Amen.

Nunc Dimíttis

Nunc dimíttis servum tuum, Dómine, secúndum verbum
    tuum, in pace:
Quia vidérunt óculi mei salutáre tuum
Quod parásti ante fáciem ómnium populórum:
Lumen ad revelatiónem géntium, et glóriam plebis tuae
    Ísrael. Amen.

Save Us, Lord

Save us, Lord, while we are awake; protect us while we sleep;
that we may keep watch with Christ and with him rest
in peace.
Let us pray.
Lord our God, after the fatigue of our daily work, renew us
by sleep, so that, always renewed by your help, we may
serve you in body and mind.
Through Christ our Lord. Amen.

A quiet night and a perfect end grant to us, Lord almighty.
Amen.

Angel of God

Angel of God,
you who are my guardian,
(this day / this night) enlighten, guard, rule, and govern
me, who am committed to you by heavenly piety.
Amen.

SALVA NOS, DÓMINE

Salva nos, Dómine, vigilántes, custódi nos dormiéntes; ut
vigilémus cum Christo et requiescámus in pace.

Orémus.
Dómine Deus noster, diúrno labóre fatigátos, quiéto sopóre
nos réfove, ut, tuo semper auxílio recreáti, tibi córpore
simus et mente devóti. Per Christum Dóminum
nostrum. Amen.

Noctem quiétam et finem perféctum concédat nobis,
Dóminus omnípotens.
Amen.

ÁNGELE DEI

Ángele Dei,
qui custos es mei,
me tibi commíssum pietáte supérna;
(Hodie / Hac nocte) illúmina, custódi, rege, et gubérna.
Amen.

Jesus Prayer

Jesus Christ, Son of God, Lord, have mercy on me, a sinner.

Act of Contrition

My God, from my whole heart I repent of all my sins, and I detest them, because by sinning I have not only justly merited the appointed penalties, but especially because they offend you, the highest good, and one worthy of being loved above all. Therefore I firmly resolve, with your grace supporting me, not to sin from now on and to flee near occasions of sin. Amen.

I Confess

(These forms are suitable for personal prayer but not liturgy.)

I confess to almighty God,
To blessed Mary ever-Virgin,
To blessed Michael the Archangel,
To blessed John the Baptist,
To the holy Apostles Peter and Paul,
and to all the saints,
that I have sinned exceedingly
in thought, word, and deed,

IESU CHRISTE

Iesu Christe, Fili Dei, Dómine, miserére mei peccatóris.

ACTUS CONTRITIÓNIS

Deus meus, ex toto corde poénitet me ómnium meórum peccatórum, éaque detéstor, quia peccándo non solum poenas a Te iuste statútas proméritus sum, sed praesértim quia offéndi Te, summum bonum, ac dignum qui super ómnia diligáris. Ideo fírmiter propóno, adiuvánte grátia Tua, de cétero me non peccatúrum peccandíque occasiónes próximas fugitúrum. Amen.

CONFÍTEOR

Confíteor Deo Omnipoténti,
beátae Maríae semper Vírgini,
beáto Michaéli Archángelo,
beáto Joánni Baptístae,
sanctis Apóstolis Petro et Paulo,
et ómnibus sanctis,
quia peccávi nimis
cogitatióne, verbo, et ópere,

through my fault, through my fault, through my most
grievous fault.
Therefore, I ask
Blessed Mary ever-Virgin,
Blessed Michael the Archangel,
Blessed John the Baptist,
the holy Apostles Peter and Paul,
and all the saints, to pray for me
to the Lord our God. Amen.

Abbreviated Form

I confess to almighty God
that I have sinned exceedingly
in thought, word,
deed, and by omission,
through my fault, through my fault, through my most
grievous fault.
Therefore, I ask
Blessed Mary ever-Virgin,
All the angels and saints,
to pray for me to the Lord our God.
Amen.

mea culpa, mea culpa,
mea máxima culpa.
Ídeo, precor
beátam Maríam semper Vírginem,
beátum Michaélem Archángelum,
beátum Joánnem Baptístam,
sanctos Apóstolos Petrum et Paulum,
omnes sanctos, oráre pro me
ad Dóminum Deum nostrum. Amen.

Forma Brevis

Confíteor Deo omnipoténti
quia peccávi nimis
cogitatióne, verbo,
ópere et omissióne,
mea culpa, mea culpa,
mea máxima culpa.
Ídeo, precor
beátam Maríam semper Vírginem,
omnes ángelos et sanctos,
oráre pro me ad Dóminum Deum nostrum.
Amen.

Prayers for Adoration and Holy Communion

O Saving Victim

O saving Victim,
you who fling open the door of heaven:
hostile forces pursue us;
give us strength; bring assistance.
To the one and triune Lord
be everlasting glory,
who life without end
gives to us in our own country.
Amen.

Down in Adoration

Therefore so great a Sacrament
let us venerate bent low:
and may the old form
yield to the new rite:
may faith stand as a supplement
for the defect of the senses.
To the Begetter and the Begotten
be praise and shouting,
salvation, honor, strength, too,
and blessing be as well:
to the One who proceeds from both
may there be the same praise.
Amen.

O Salutáris Hóstia

O salutáris Hóstia,
Quae caeli pandis óstium:
Bella premunt hostília;
Da robur; fer auxílium.
Uni trinóque Dómino
Sit sempitérna glória,
Qui vitam sine término
Nobis donet in pátria.
Amen.

Tantum Ergo

Tantum ergo Sacraméntum
Venerémur cérnui:
Et antíquum documéntum
Novo cedat rítui:
Praestet fides suppleméntum
Sénsuum deféctui.
Genitóri, Genitóque
Laus et iubilátio,
Salus, honor, virtus quoque
Sit et benedíctio:
Procedénti ab utróque
Compar sit laudátio.
Amen.

Divine Praises

Blessed be God.
Blessed be his holy Name.
Blessed be Jesus Christ, true God and true Man.
Blessed be the Name of Jesus.
Blessed be his most sacred Heart.
Blessed be his most precious Blood.
Blessed be Jesus in the most holy Sacrament of the altar.
Blessed be the Holy Spirit, the Paraclete.
Blessed be the exalted Mother of God, the most holy Mary.
Blessed be her holy and immaculate Conception.
Blessed be her glorious Assumption.
Blessed be the name of Mary, Virgin and Mother.
Blessed be the holy Joseph, her most chaste Spouse.
Blessed be God in his angels and in his saints.
Amen.

Laudes Divínae

Benedíctus Deus.
Benedíctus Nomen Sanctum eius.
Benedíctus Iesus Christus, verus Deus et verus Homo.
Benedíctum Nomen Iesu.
Benedíctum Cor eius sacratíssimum.
Benedíctus Sanguis eius pretiosíssimus.
Benedíctus Iesus in sanctíssimo altáris Sacraménto.
Benedíctus Sanctus Spíritus, Paraclítus.
Benedícta excélsa Mater Dei, María sanctíssima.
Benedícta sancta eius et immaculáta Concéptio.
Benedícta eius gloriósa Assúmptio.
Benedíctum nomen Maríae, Vírginis et Matris.
Benedíctus sanctus Ioseph, eius castíssimus Sponsus.
Benedíctus Deus in ángelis suis, et in sanctis suis.
Amen.

SOUL OF CHRIST

Soul of Christ, sanctify me.
Body of Christ, save me.
Blood of Christ, intoxicate me.
Water of the side of Christ, wash me.
Suffering of Christ, comfort me.
O good Jesus, listen to me.
Within your wounds hide me.
Do not allow me to be separated from you.
From the wicked enemy defend me.
In the hour of my death call me,
and command me to come to you,
so that with your saints I may praise you
into the ages of ages.
Amen.

ÁNIMA CHRISTI

Ánima Christi, sanctífica me.
Corpus Christi, salva me.
Sanguis Christi, inébria me.
Aqua láteris Christi, lava me.
Pássio Christi, confórta me.
O bone Iesu, exaúdi me.
Intra tua vúlnera abscónde me.
Ne permíttas me separári a te.
Ab hoste malígno defénde me.
In hora mortis meae voca me,
Et iube me veníre ad te,
Ut cum sanctis tuis laudem te
In saécula saeculórum.
Amen.

AFTER HOLY COMMUNION

I give you thanks, Lord, holy Father, almighty eternal God, who have deemed me, a sinner, your unworthy servant—through no merit of mine, but only by the kindness of your mercy—worthy to satisfy myself with the precious Body and Blood of your Son, our Lord Jesus Christ. And I pray that this holy communion may not be a charge for punishment to me, but healthy intercession for forgiveness. May it be to me armor of faith and a shield of good will. May it be an emptying out of my vices, a banishment of my concupiscence and lust, and an increase in charity and patience, humility and obedience, and all the virtues: against the schemes of all enemies, visible as well as invisible, a firm defense; of my disturbances, bodily as well as spiritual, a perfect calming; to you, the one and true God, a firm link; and the end of my happy fulfilment. And I pray you, that to that ineffable banquet you will condescend to lead me, a sinner, where you, with your Son and the Holy Spirit, are the true light of your saints, full of abundance, eternal joy, complete delight, and perfect happiness. Through the same Christ our Lord. Amen.

Grátias Tibi Ago

Grátias tibi ago, Dómine, sancte Pater, omnípotens aetérne Deus, qui me peccatórem, indígnum fámulum tuum—nullis meis méritis, sed sola dignatióne misericórdiae tuae—satiáre dignátus es pretióso Córpore et Sánguine Fílii tui, Dómini nostri Iesu Christi. Et precor ut haec sancta commúnio non sit mihi reátus ad poenam, sed intercéssio salutáris ad véniam. Sit mihi armatúra fídei et scutum bonae voluntátis. Sit vitiórum meórum evacuátio, concupiscéntiae et libídinis exterminátio, caritátis et patiéntiae, humilitátis et oboediéntiae, omniúmque virtútum augmentátio: contra insídias inimicórum ómnium, tam visibílium quam invisibílium, firma defénsio; mótuum meórum, tam carnálium quam spirituálium, perfécta quietátio; in te uno ac vero Deo firma adhaésio; atque finis mei felix consummátio. Et precor te, ut ad illud ineffábile convívium me peccatórem perdúcere dígneris, ubi tu, cum Fílio tuo et Spíritu Sancto, sanctis tuis es lux vera, satíetas plena, gaúdium sempitérnum, iucúnditas consummáta et felícitas perfécta. Per eúndem Christum Dóminum nostrum. Amen.

HAIL, TRUE BODY

Hail, true body, born of the Virgin Mary,
Who having truly suffered, was sacrificed on the cross for
    humankind,
from whose pieced side flowed water and blood:
May it be for us a foretaste in the trial of death.
O sweet Jesus, O holy Jesus,
O Jesus, Son of Mary.
Amen.

Ave Verum Corpus

Ave, verum corpus, natum de María Vírgine,
Vere passum, immolátum in cruce pro hómine,

Cuius latus perforátum fluxit aqua et sánguine:
Esto nobis praegustátum mortis in exámine.
O Iesu dulcis, O Iesu pie,
O Iesu, fili Maríae.
Amen.

Prayers of the Rosary

Sign of the Cross

In the name of the Father, and of the Son, and of the Holy Spirit. Amen.

Apostles' Creed

I believe in God the Father almighty, Creator of heaven and earth. And in Jesus Christ, his only Son, our Lord, who was conceived by the Holy Spirit, born from the Virgin Mary, suffered under Pontius Pilate, was crucified, died, and was buried; who descended to the underworld; who on the third day rose again from the dead; who ascended to heaven, is seated at the right hand of God the Father almighty; who is to come again to judge the living and the dead. I believe in the Holy Spirit, the holy catholic Church, the communion of saints, the forgiveness of sins, the resurrection of the flesh, eternal life. Amen.

Our Father

Our Father, you who are in heaven, may your name be made holy. May your kingdom come. May your will be done, as in heaven, so also on earth. Our daily bread give us this day, and forgive us our debts, as we also forgive the debts of our debtors. And do not lead us into temptation, but free us from evil. Amen.

SIGNUM CRUCIS

In nómine Patris, et Fílii, et Spíritus Sancti. Amen.

SÝMBOLUM APOSTOLÓRUM

Credo in Deum Patrem omnipoténtem, Creatórem caeli et terrae. Et in Iesum Christum, Fílium eius únicum, Dóminum nostrum, qui concéptus est de Spíritu Sancto, natus ex María Vírgine, passus sub Póntio Piláto, crucifíxus, mórtuus, et sepúltus; descéndit ad ínfernos; tértia die resurréxit a mórtuis; ascéndit ad caelos, sedet ad déxteram Dei Patris omnipoténtis; inde ventúrus est iudicáre vivos et mórtuos. Credo in Spíritum Sanctum, sanctam Ecclésiam cathólicam, sanctórum communiónem, remissiónem peccatórum, carnis resurrectiónem, vitam aetérnam. Amen.

PATER NOSTER

Pater noster, qui es in caelis, sanctificétur nomen tuum. Advéniat regnum tuum. Fiat volúntas tua, sicut in caelo, et in terra. Panem nostrum quotidiánum da nobis hódie, et dimítte nobis débita nostra sicut et nos dimíttimus debitóribus nostris. Et ne nos indúcas in tentatiónem, sed líbera nos a malo. Amen.

Hail Mary

Hail Mary, full of grace, the Lord is with you. Blessed are you among women, and blessed is the fruit of your womb, Jesus. Holy Mary, Mother of God, pray for us sinners, now and in the hour of our death. Amen.

Glory Be

Glory to the Father, and to the Son, and to the Holy Spirit. As it was in the beginning, and now, and always, and into the ages of ages. Amen.

Fatima Prayer

O my Jesus, forgive us our debts, save us from the fire below, lead all souls through to heaven, especially those who most need your mercy. Amen.

Mysteries of the Rosary

Joyful Mysteries

1. The Annunciation
2. The Visitation

AVE MARÍA

Ave María, grátia plena, Dóminus tecum. Benedícta tu in muliéribus, et benedíctus fructus ventris tui, Iesus. Sancta María, Mater Dei, ora pro nobis peccatóribus, nunc, et in hora mortis nostrae. Amen.

GLÓRIA PATRI

Glória Patri, et Fílio, et Spirítui Sancto. Sicut erat in princípio, et nunc, et semper, et in saécula saeculórum. Amen.

ORÁTIO FÁTIMA

O mi Iesu, dimítte nobis débita nostra, salva nos ab igne inferióri, perduc in caelum omnes ánimas, praesértim eas, quae misericórdiae tuae máxime índigent. Amen.

MYSTÉRIA ROSÁRII

Mystéria Gaudiósa

1. Annuntiátio
2. Visitátio

3. The Nativity

4. The Presentation

5. The Finding in the Temple

Sorrowful Mysteries

1. The Agony in the Garden

2. The Scourging

3. The Crowning with Thorns

4. The Carrying of the Cross

5. The Crucifixion and Death

Glorious Mysteries

1. The Resurrection

2. The Ascension

3. The Descent of the Holy Spirit

4. The Assumption

5. The Coronation in Heaven

~~*Luminous Mysteries*~~

~~1. The Baptism of the Lord~~

~~2. The Wedding at Cana~~

~~3. The Proclamation of God's Kingdom~~

~~4. The Transfiguration~~

~~5. The Institution of the Eucharist~~

3. Natívitas

4. Praesentátio

5. Invéntio in Templo

Mystéria Dolorósa

1. Agonía in Hortu

2. Flagellátio

3. Coronátio Spinis

4. Baiulátio Crucis

5. Crucifíxio et Mors

Mystéria Gloriósa

1. Resurréctio

2. Ascénsio

3. Descénsus Spíritus Sancti

4. Assúmptio

5. Coronátio in Caelo

Mystéria Luminósa

1. Baptísma Dómini

2. Núptiae Canénses

3. Proclamátio Regni Dei

4. Transfigurátio

5. Institútio Eucharístiae

Hail, Holy Queen

Hail Queen, Mother of mercy;
our life, sweetness, and hope, hail.
To you we cry, exiled children of Eve;
to you we sigh, groaning and weeping in
    this valley of tears.
Come, therefore, our Advocate,
turn those merciful eyes of yours toward us;
and show us Jesus, the blessed fruit of your womb, after this
    exile.
O merciful, O pious, O sweet Virgin Mary.
Amen.

V. Pray for us, holy Bearer of God,
R. *So that we may be made worthy of the promises of Christ.*

Concluding Prayers

Let us pray.

God, whose Only-Begotten through his life, death, and resurrection has bought for us the rewards of eternal salvation: grant, we beg, that, reflecting on these mysteries of the blessed Virgin Mary by means of the Rosary, we may both imitate what they contain and reach what they promise. Through the same Christ our Lord. Amen.

Salve Regína

Salve Regína, Mater misericórdiae;
Vita, dulcédo, et spes nostra, salve.
Ad te clamámus, éxsules fílii Evae;
Ad te suspirámus, geméntes et flentes in hac lacrimárum
  valle.
Eia ergo, Advocáta nostra,
Illos tuos misericórdes óculos ad nos convérte;
Et Iesum, benedíctum fructum ventris tui, nobis post hoc
  exsílium osténde.
O clemens, o pia, o dulcis Virgo María.
Amen.

V. Ora pro nobis, Sancta Dei Génetrix.
R. *Ut digni efficiámur promissiónibus Christi.*

Oratiónes ad Finem

Orémus.

Deus, cuius Unigénitus per vitam, mortem, et
resurrectiónem suam nobis salútis aetérnae praémia
comparávit: concéde, quaésumus, ut haec mystéria
sacratíssimo beátae Maríae Vírginis Rosário recoléntes, et
imitémur quod cóntinent et quod promíttunt, assequámur.
Per eúndem Chrístum Dóminum nostrum. Amen.

Prayers Used in St. Louis de Montfort's Consecration to Mary

Prayers not included were originally written in French.

Come, Creator Spirit

Come, Creator Spirit,
visit your minds,
fill with heavenly grace
the hearts that you have created.

You who are called the Paraclete,
the gift of God most high,
living source, fire, love,
and anointing of the spirit.

You, sevenfold in gift,
the finger of the paternal right hand,
you, duly sent forth of the Father,
enriching our throat with your word.

Kindle a light for our senses,
pour out love for our hearts,
making the infirmity of our body
by your strength firm to endure.

May you drive the enemy far away
and give peace forever;
thus with you as leader showing the way
we will avoid every harm.

Grant us that through you we may know the Father
and be familiar with the Son,

VENI CREÁTOR

Veni Creátor Spíritus,
mentes tuórum vísita,
imple supérna grátia,
quae tu creásti, péctora.

Qui díceris Paráclitus,
altíssimi donum Dei,
fons vivus, ignis, cáritas,
et spiritális únctio.

Tu septifórmis múnere,
dígitus patérnae déxterae,
tu rite promíssum Patris,
sermóne ditans gúttura.

Accénde lumen sénsibus,
infúnde amórem córdibus,
infirma nostri córporis
virtúte firmans pérpeti.

Hostem repéllas lóngius
pacémque dones prótinus;
ductóre sic te praévio
vitémus omne nóxium.

Per te sciámus da Patrem
noscámus atque Fílium,

and that we may believe in you,
the Spirit of both, through all time.
Amen. (Alleluia.)

HAIL, STAR OF THE SEA

Hail, star of the sea,
nourishing mother of God,
also ever Virgin,
happy gate of heaven.

Taking up that "Hail"
from Gabriel's mouth,
establish us in peace,
altering the name of Eve.
*[This is an untranslatable pun. "Hail" is "Ave." The Latin form
of "Eve" is "Eva," which is "Ave" backward.]*

Break the chains for the prisoners,
bring out light for the blind,
beat away our ills,
beg for all good things.

Show yourself to be a mother;
may he take up, through you, our prayers
who, born for us,
has taken on himself to be yours.

teque utriúsque Spíritum
credámus omni témpore.
Amen. (Allelúia.)

AVE MARIS STELLA

Ave, maris stella,
Dei mater alma,
atque semper virgo,
felix coeli porta.

Sumens illud "Ave"
Gabriélis ore,
funda nos in pace,
mutans Evae nomen.

Solve vincla reis,
profer lumen caecis,
mala nostra pelle,
bona cuncta posce.

Monstra te esse matrem;
sumat per te preces
qui pro nobis natus
tulit esse tuus.

Virgin unique,
mild above all,
Make us, loosed from sins,
mild and chaste.

Present a pure life,
prepare a safe way,
so that, seeing Jesus,
we may always rejoice together.

Praise be to God the Father,
To the most high Christ, glory,
to the Holy Spirit,
honor, one in three. Amen.

Virgo singuláris,
inter omnes mitis,
nos, culpis solútos,
mites fac et castos.

Vitam praesta puram,
iter para tutum,
ut vidéntes Iesum
semper collaetémur.

Sit laus Deo Patri,
summo Christo decus,
Spiritúi Sancto,
tribus honor unus.

Canticle of Mary

My soul glorifies the Lord,
and my spirit has rejoiced in God my savior,
because he has paid attention to the humility of his
   handmaid.
For behold, from now on all generations will call me blessed,
because he who is mighty has done great things for me, and
   holy is his name,
and his mercy belongs to those who fear him, from generation to generation.
He has shown might in his arm; he has scattered the proud
   in the thoughts of their hearts.
He has thrust the powerful from their seats and exalted the
   humble.
The hungry he has filled with good things, and the rich he
   has sent away empty.
He has raised up Israel his servant, remembering his mercy,
as he spoke to our fathers, to Abraham and his seed forever.
Amen.

Glory Be

Glory to the Father, and to the Son, and to the Holy Spirit.
As it was in the beginning, and now, and always, and into
the ages of ages. Amen.

MAGNÍFICAT

Magníficat ánima mea Dóminum,
Et exultávit spíritus meus in Deo salutári meo,
Quia respéxit humilitátem ancíllae suae.

Ecce enim ex hoc beátam me dicent omnes generatiónes,
Quia fécit mihi mágna qui pótens est, et sánctum nómen eius.

Et misericórdia eius in progénies et progénies timéntibus
eum.
Fécit poténtiam in bráchio suo; dispérsit supérbos mente
cordis sui.
Depósuit poténtes de sede et exaltávit húmiles.

Esuriéntes implévit bonis, et dívites dimísit inánes.

Suscépit Ísrael púerum suum, recordátus misericórdiae suae.
Sicut locútus est ad patres nostros, Ábraham, et sémini eius
in saécula.
Amen.

GLÓRIA PATRI

Glória Patri, et Fílio, et Spirítui Sancto. Sicut erat in princípio,
et nunc, et semper, et in saécula saeculórum. Amen.

Litany of Loreto

Lord, have mercy. *Lord, have mercy.*
Christ, have mercy. *Christ, have mercy.*
Lord, have mercy. *Lord, have mercy.*
Christ, hear us. *Christ, listen to us.*
God, the Father of heaven,
Have mercy on us.
God the Son, Redeemer of the World,
Have mercy on us.
God the Holy Spirit,
Have mercy on us.
Holy Trinity, one God,
Have mercy on us.
Holy Mary,
Pray for us.
Holy Bearer of God,
Pray for us.
Holy Virgin of virgins,
Pray for us.
Mother of Christ,
Pray for us.
Mother of the Church,
Pray for us.
Mother of mercy,
Pray for us.
Mother of divine grace,
Pray for us.
Mother of hope,
Pray for us.

LITÁNIAE LAURÉTANAE

Kýrie, eléison. *Kýrie, eléison.*
Christe, eléison. *Christe, eléison.*
Kýrie, eléison. *Kýrie, eléison.*
Christe, audi nos. *Christe, exaúdi nos.*
Pater de caelis, Deus,
Miserére nobis.
Fili, Redémptor mundi, Deus,
Miserére nobis.
Spíritus Sancte, Deus,
Miserére nobis.
Sancta Trínitas, unus Deus,
Miserére nobis.
Sancta Maria,
Ora pro nobis.
Sancta Dei Génitrix,
Ora pro nobis.
Sancta Virgo vírginum,
Ora pro nobis.
Mater Christi,
Ora pro nobis.
Mater Ecclésia,
Ora pro nobis.
Mater misericórdia,
Ora pro nobis.
Mater divínae grátiae,
Ora pro nobis.
Mater spei,
Ora pro nobis.

Most pure Mother,
Pray for us.
Most chaste Mother,
Pray for us.
Inviolate Mother,
Pray for us.
Undefiled Mother,
Pray for us.
Lovable Mother,
Pray for us.
Admirable Mother,
Pray for us.
Mother of good counsel,
Pray for us.
Mother of the Creator,
Pray for us.
Mother of the Savior,
Pray for us.
Most prudent Virgin,
Pray for us.
Venerable Virgin,
Pray for us.
Illustrious Virgin,
Pray for us.
Powerful Virgin,
Pray for us.
Merciful Virgin,
Pray for us.
Faithful Virgin,
Pray for us.

Mater puríssima,
Ora pro nobis.
Mater castíssima,
Ora pro nobis.
Mater invioláta,
Ora pro nobis.
Mater intemeráta,
Ora pro nobis.
Mater amábilis,
Ora pro nobis.
Mater admirábilis,
Ora pro nobis.
Mater boni consílii,
Ora pro nobis.
Mater Creatóris,
Ora pro nobis.
Mater Salvatóris,
Ora pro nobis.
Virgo prudentíssima,
Ora pro nobis.
Virgo veneránda,
Ora pro nobis.
Virgo praedicánda,
Ora pro nobis.
Virgo potens,
Ora pro nobis.
Virgo clemens,
Ora pro nobis.
Virgo fidélis,
Ora pro nobis.

Mirror of justice,
Pray for us.
Seat of wisdom,
Pray for us.
Cause of our joy,
Pray for us.
Spiritual vessel,
Pray for us.
Honorable vessel,
Pray for us.
Distinguished vessel of devotion,
Pray for us.
Mystic Rose,
Pray for us.
Tower of David,
Pray for us.
Ivory tower,
Pray for us.
Golden house,
Pray for us.
Ark of the Covenant,
Pray for us.
Gate of heaven,
Pray for us.
Morning star,
Pray for us.
Health of the sick,
Pray for us.
Refuge of sinners,
Pray for us.

Spéculum iustítiae,
Ora pro nobis.
Sedes sapiéntiae,
Ora pro nobis.
Causa nostrae laetítiae,
Ora pro nobis.
Vas spirituále,
Ora pro nobis.
Vas honorábile,
Ora pro nobis.
Vas insígne devotiónis,
Ora pro nobis.
Rosa mýstica,
Ora pro nobis.
Turris Davídica,
Ora pro nobis.
Turris ebúrnea,
Ora pro nobis.
Domus aúrea,
Ora pro nobis.
Foéderis arca,
Ora pro nobis.
Iánua coeli,
Ora pro nobis.
Stella matútina,
Ora pro nobis.
Salus infirmórum,
Ora pro nobis.
Refúgium peccatórum,
Ora pro nobis.

Comfort of migrants,
Pray for us.
Consoler of the afflicted,
Pray for us.
Help of Christians,
Pray for us.
Queen of the Angels,
Pray for us.
Queen of the Patriarchs,
Pray for us.
Queen of the Prophets,
Pray for us.
Queen of the Apostles,
Pray for us.
Queen of the Martyrs,
Pray for us.
Queen of the Confessors,
Pray for us.
Queen of Virgins,
Pray for us.
Queen of all Saints,
Pray for us.
Queen without original sin conceived,
Pray for us.
Queen assumed into heaven,
Pray for us.
Queen of the Most Holy Rosary,
Pray for us.
Queen of the family,
Pray for us.

Solácium migrántium,
Ora pro nobis.
Consolátrix afflictórum,
Ora pro nobis.
Auxílium Christianórum,
Ora pro nobis.
Regína Angelórum,
Ora pro nobis.
Regína Patriarchárum,
Ora pro nobis.
Regína Prophetárum,
Ora pro nobis.
Regína Apostolórum,
Ora pro nobis.
Regína Mártyrum,
Ora pro nobis.
Regína Confessórum,
Ora pro nobis.
Regína Vírginum,
Ora pro nobis.
Regína Sanctórum ómnium,
Ora pro nobis.
Regína sine labe origináli concépta,
Ora pro nobis.
Regína in caelum assúmpta,
Ora pro nobis.
Regína Sacratíssimi Rosárii,
Ora pro nobis.
Regína famíliae,
Ora pro nobis.

Queen of peace.
Pray for us.

Lamb of God, you who take away the sins of the world,
Spare us, Lord.
Lamb of God, you who take away the sins of the world,
Listen to us, Lord.
Lamb of God, you who take away the sins of the world,
Have mercy on us.
Christ, hear us.
Christ, listen to us.
V. Pray for us, holy Bearer of God,
R. That we may be made worthy of the promises of Christ.
Let us pray.

We beg, Lord, fill our minds with your grace; so that we who have come to know the Incarnation of Christ your Son by the angel's announcement, through his Suffering and Cross may be led through to the glory of the resurrection. Through the same Christ our Lord.
R. Amen.
V. May the divine help remain always with us.
R. Amen.

Litany of the Holy Name of Jesus

Lord, have mercy. *Christ, have mercy.*
Lord, have mercy.
Jesus, hear us. *Jesus, listen to us.*
God, the Father of heaven,
Have mercy on us.

Regína pacis,
Ora pro nobis.

Agnus Dei, qui tollis peccáta mundi,
Parce nobis, Domine.
Agnus Dei, qui tollis peccáta mundi,
Exaúdi nos, Domine.
Agnus Dei, qui tollis peccáta mundi,
Miserére nobis.
Christe, audi nos.
Christe, exaúdi nos.
V. Ora pro nobis, sancta Dei Génitrix.
R. Ut digni efficiámur promissiónibus Christi.
Orémus.

Grátiam tuam, quaésumus Dómine, méntibus nostris infúnde; ut qui, ángelo nuntiánte Christi Fílii tui Incarnatiónem cognóvimus, per Passiónem eius et Crucem ad resurrectiónis glóriam perducámur. Per eúndem Christum Dóminum nostrum.
R. Amen.
V. Divínum auxílium máneat semper nobíscum.
R. Amen.

Litániae Sanctíssimi Nóminis Iesu

Kýrie, eléison. *Christe, eléison.*
Kýrie, eléison.
Iesu, audi nos. *Iesu, exaúdi nos.*
Pater de caelis, Deus,
Miserére nobis.

God the Son, Redeemer of the world,
Have mercy on us.
God, the Holy Spirit,
Have mercy on us.
Holy Trinity, one God,
Have mercy on us.
Jesus, Son of the living God,
Have mercy on us.
Jesus, splendor of the Father,
Have mercy on us.
Jesus, brightness of eternal light,
Have mercy on us.
Jesus, king of glory,
Have mercy on us.
Jesus, sun of justice,
Have mercy on us.
Jesus, Son of the Virgin Mary,
Have mercy on us.
Jesus, lovable one,
Have mercy on us.
Jesus, admirable one,
Have mercy on us.
Jesus, strong God,
Have mercy on us.
Jesus, father of the age to come,
Have mercy on us.
Jesus, angel of great counsel,
Have mercy on us.
Jesus, most powerful one,
Have mercy on us.

Fili, Redémptor mundi, Deus,
Miserére nobis.
Spíritus Sancte, Deus,
Miserére nobis.
Sancta Trínitas, unus Deus,
Miserére nobis.
Iesu, Fili Dei vivi,
Miserére nobis.
Iesu, splendor Patris,
Miserére nobis.
Iesu, candor lucis aetérnae,
Miserére nobis.
Iesu, rex glóriae,
Miserére nobis.
Iesu, sol iustítiae,
Miserére nobis.
Iesu, Fili Maríae Vírginis,
Miserére nobis.
Iesu, amábilis,
Miserére nobis.
Iesu, admirábilis,
Miserére nobis.
Iesu, Deus fortis,
Miserére nobis.
Iesu, pater futúri saéculi,
Miserére nobis.
Iesu, magni consílii ángele,
Miserére nobis.
Iesu, potentíssime,
Miserére nobis.

Jesus, most patient one,
Have mercy on us.
Jesus, most obedient one,
Have mercy on us.
Jesus, gentle and humble in heart,
Have mercy on us.
Jesus, lover of chastity,
Have mercy on us.
Jesus, our lover,
Have mercy on us.
Jesus, God of peace,
Have mercy on us.
Jesus, author of life,
Have mercy on us.
Jesus, pattern of the virtues,
Have mercy on us.
Jesus, zealous for our souls,
Have mercy on us.
Jesus, our God,
Have mercy on us.
Jesus, our refuge,
Have mercy on us.
Jesus, father of the poor,
Have mercy on us.
Jesus, treasury of the faithful,
Have mercy on us.
Jesus, good shepherd,
Have mercy on us.
Jesus, true light,
Have mercy on us.

Iesu, patientíssime,
Miserére nobis.
Iesu, oboedientíssime,
Miserére nobis.
Iesu, mitis et húmilis corde,
Miserére nobis.
Iesu, amátor castitítis,
Miserére nobis.
Iesu, amátor noster,
Miserére nobis.
Iesu, Deus pacis,
Miserére nobis.
Iesu, auctor vitae,
Miserére nobis.
Iesu, exémplar virtútum,
Miserére nobis.
Iesu, zelátor animarum,
Miserére nobis.
Iesu, Deus noster,
Miserére nobis.
Iesu, refúgium nostrum,
Miserére nobis.
Iesu, pater paúperum,
Miserére nobis.
Iesu, thesaúre fidélium,
Miserére nobis.
Iesu, bone pastor,
Miserére nobis.
Iesu, lux vera,
Miserére nobis.

Jesus, eternal wisdom,
Have mercy on us.
Jesus, unbounded goodness,
Have mercy on us.
Jesus, our way and life,
Have mercy on us.
Jesus, joy of the angels,
Have mercy on us.
Jesus, king of the patriarchs,
Have mercy on us.
Jesus, master of the apostles,
Have mercy on us.
Jesus, teacher of the evangelists,
Have mercy on us.
Jesus, courage of the martyrs,
Have mercy on us.
Jesus, light of the confessors,
Have mercy on us.
Jesus, purity of virgins,
Have mercy on us.
Jesus, crown of all the saints,
Have mercy on us.
Be favorable. *Spare us, Jesus.*
Be favorable. *Listen to us, Jesus.*
From every evil,
Free us, Jesus.
From every sin,
Free us, Jesus.
From your wrath,
Free us, Jesus.

Iesu, sapiéntia aeterna,
Miserére nobis.
Iesu, bónitas infínita,
Miserére nobis.
Iesu, via et vita nostra,
Miserére nobis.
Iesu, gaúdium angelórum,
Miserére nobis.
Iesu, rex patriarchárum,
Miserére nobis.
Iesu, mágister apostolórum,
Miserére nobis.
Iesu, doctor evangelistárum,
Miserére nobis.
Iesu, fortitúdo mártyrum,
Miserére nobis.
Iesu, lumen confessórum,
Miserére nobis.
Iesu, púritas vírginum,
Miserére nobis.
Iesu, coróna sanctórum ómnium,
Miserére nobis.
Propítius esto. *Parce nobis, Iesu.*
Propítius esto. *Exaudi nos, Iesu.*
Ab omni malo,
Líbera nos, Iesu.
Ab omni peccáto,
Líbera nos, Iesu.
Ab ira tua,
Líbera nos, Iesu.

From the schemes of the devil,
Free us, Jesus.
From a spirit of fornication,
Free us, Jesus.
From perpetual death,
Free us, Jesus.
From neglect of your inspirations,
Free us, Jesus.
Through the mystery of your holy Incarnation,
Free us, Jesus.
Through your nativity,
Free us, Jesus.
Through your childhood,
Free us, Jesus.
Through your most divine life,
Free us, Jesus.
Through your labors,
Free us, Jesus.
Through your agony and suffering,
Free us, Jesus.
Through your cross and abandonment,
Free us, Jesus.
Through your fatigues,
Free us, Jesus.
Through your death and tomb,
Free us, Jesus.
Through your resurrection,
Free us, Jesus.
Through your ascension,
Free us, Jesus.

Ab insídiis diáboli,
Líbera nos, Iesu.
A spíritu fornicátionis,
Líbera nos, Iesu.
A morte perpétua,
Líbera nos, Iesu.
A negléctu inspiratiónum tuárum,
Líbera nos, Iesu.
Per mystérium sanctae Incarnatiónis tuae,
Líbera nos, Iesu.
Per nativitátem tuam,
Líbera nos, Iesu.
Per infántiam tuam,
Líbera nos, Iesu.
Per diviníssimam vitam tuam,
Líbera nos, Iesu.
Per labóres tuos,
Líbera nos, Iesu.
Per agóniam et passiónem tuam,
Líbera nos, Iesu.
Per crucem et derelictiónem tuam,
Líbera nos, Iesu.
Per languóres tuos,
Líbera nos, Iesu.
Per mortem et sepultúram tuam,
Líbera nos, Iesu.
Per resurrectiónem tuam,
Líbera nos, Iesu.
Per ascensiónem tuam,
Líbera nos, Iesu.

Through your institution of the most holy Eucharist,
Free us, Jesus.
Through your joy,
Free us, Jesus.
Through your glory,
Free us, Jesus.
Lamb of God, you who take away the sins of the world,
Spare us, Lord.
Lamb of God, you who take away the sins of the world,
Listen to us, Jesus.
Lamb of God, you who take away the sins of the world,
Have mercy on us, Jesus.
Jesus, hear us. *Jesus, listen to us.*
Let us pray.

Lord Jesus Christ, who said: Ask, and you will receive; seek, and you will find; knock, and it will be opened for you: we beg you, give us who are asking the compassion of your most divine love, so that with our whole heart, mouth, and works we may love you and may never cease from your praise. Cause us to have, Lord, equally a perpetual fear and love of your holy name, because you never leave without your leadership those whom you establish in the firmness of your love. Who live and reign into the ages of ages. Amen.

O Jesus, Living in Mary

O Jesus, living in Mary, come and live in your servants, in the Spirit of your holiness, in the fullness of your strength,

Per sanctíssimae Eucharístiae institutiónem tuam,
Líbera nos, Iesu.
Per gaúdia tua,
Líbera nos, Iesu.
Per glóriam tuam,
Líbera nos, Iesu.
Agnus Dei, qui tollis peccáta mundi,
  Parce nobis, Domine.
Agnus Dei, qui tollis peccáta mundi,
  Exaúdi nos, Iesu.
Agnus Dei, qui tollis peccáta mundi,
  Miserére nobis, Iesu.
Iesu, audi nos. *Iesu, exaúdi nos.*
Orémus.

Dómine Iesu Christe, qui dixísti: Pétite, et accipiétis; quáerite, et inveniétis; pulsáte, et aperiétur vobis: quáesumus, da nobis peténtibus diviníssimi tui amóris afféctum, ut te toto corde, ore et ópere diligámus, et a tua nunquam láude cessémus. Sancti nóminis tui, Dómine, timórem páriter et amórem fac nos habére perpétuum, quia nunquam tua gubernatióne destítuis quos in soliditáte túae dilectiónis instítuis. Qui vivis et regnas in saécula saeculórum. Amen.

O Iesu, Vivens in María

O Iesu, vivens in María, veni et vive in fámulis tuis, in Spíritus sanctitátis tuae, in plenitúdine virtútis tuae, in

in the truth of your virtues, in the perfection of your ways, in your mysterious communion, be master of every enemy power, in your Spirit, to the glory of the Father. Amen.

veritáte virtútum tuárum, in perfectióne viárum tuárum, in communióne mysteriórum tuórum, domináre omni advérsae potestáte in Spíritu tuo ad glóriam Patris. Amen.

Prayers of the Stations of the Cross

We Adore You, O Christ

(Prayed before each Station.)
We adore you, Christ,
and bless you,
because through your holy cross
you have redeemed the world.
You who suffered for us,
Lord, Lord, have mercy on us.
Amen.

Stations of the Cross

1. Where Christ is condemned to death.
2. Where the cross is laid on Christ.
3. Where Christ first falls beneath the cross.
4. Where the Blessed Virgin, with St. John, meets Christ.
5. Where the cross is laid on Simon of Cyrene.
6. Where Veronica meets Christ.
7. Where Christ falls beneath the gate of judgment.
8. Where the women weep for Christ.
9. Where he falls for the last time at the Mount of Calvary.
10. Where he is given gall and vinegar to drink.
11. Where he is fixed to the cross by horrible nails.
12. Where he dies on the cross.
13. Where Jesus' body from the cross is laid on the knees of his afflicted mother.
14. Where Jesus' body is buried.

ADORÁMUS TE, CHRISTE

Adorámus te, Christe,
et benedícimus tibi,
quia per sanctam crucem tuam
redemísti mundum.
Qui passus es pro nobis,
Dómine, Dómine, miserére nobis.
Amen.

VIA CRUCIS

1. Ubi Christus morti adiudicátur.
2. Ubi Christo crux impónitur.
3. Ubi primum Christus sub cruce cécidit.
4. Ubi Beáta Virgo cum Sancto Ioánne óbviat Christo.
5. Ubi Simóni Cyrneaéo crux impónitur.
6. Ubi Verónica Christo óbviat.
7. Ubi Christus sub iudicária porta cécidit.
8. Ubi mulíeres Christum deplórant.
9. Ubi último cecídit ad Montem Calváriae.
10. Ubi felle et acéto potátur.
11. Ubi crucis horréndis clavis affígitur.
12. Ubi in cruce móritur.
13. Ubi Iesu corpus e cruce super afflíctae matris génua depónitur.
14. Ubi Iesu corpus sepélitur.

OUR FATHER

(Prayed after each Station)

Our Father, you who are in heaven, may your name be made holy. May your kingdom come. May your will be done, as in heaven, so also on earth. Our daily bread give us this day, and forgive our debts, as we also forgive the debts of our debtors. And do not lead us into temptation, but free us from evil. Amen.

PATER NOSTER

Pater noster, qui es in caelis, sanctificétur nomen tuum. Advéniat regnum tuum. Fiat volúntas tua, sicut in caelo, et in terra. Panem nostrum quotidiánum da nobis hódie, et dimítte nobis débita nostra sicut et nos dimíttimus debitóribus nostris. Et ne nos indúcas in tentatiónem, sed líbera nos a malo. Amen.

Prayers of the Divine Mercy Chaplet

Our Father

Our Father, you who are in heaven, may your name be made holy. May your kingdom come. May your will be done, as in heaven, so also on earth. Our daily bread give us this day, and forgive our debts, as we also forgive the debts of our debtors. And do not lead us into temptation, but free us from evil. Amen.

Hail Mary

Hail Mary, full of grace, the Lord is with you. Blessed are you among women, and blessed is the fruit of your womb, Jesus. Holy Mary, Mother of God, pray for us sinners, now and in the hour of our death. Amen.

Apostles' Creed

I believe in God the Father almighty, Creator of heaven and earth. And in Jesus Christ, his only Son, our Lord, who was conceived by the Holy Spirit, born from the Virgin Mary, suffered under Pontius Pilate, was crucified, died, and was buried; who descended to the underworld; who on the third day rose again from the dead; who ascended to heaven, is seated at the right hand of God the Father almighty; who is to come again to judge the living and the dead. I believe in the Holy Spirit, the holy catholic Church, the communion of saints, the forgiveness of sins, the resurrection of the flesh, eternal life. Amen.

PATER NOSTER

Pater noster, qui es in caelis, sanctificétur nomen tuum. Advéniat regnum tuum. Fiat volúntas tua, sicut in caelo, et in terra. Panem nostrum quotidiánum da nobis hódie, et dimítte nobis débita nostra sicut et nos dimíttimus debitóribus nostris. Et ne nos indúcas in tentatiónem, sed líbera nos a malo. Amen.

AVE MARÍA

Ave María, grátia plena, Dóminus tecum. Benedícta tu in muliéribus, et benedíctus fructus ventris tui, Iesus. Sancta María, Mater Dei, ora pro nobis peccatóribus, nunc, et in hora mortis nostrae. Amen.

SÝMBOLUM APOSTOLÓRUM

Credo in Deum Patrem omnipoténtem, Creatórem caeli et terrae. Et in Iesum Christum, Fílium eius únicum, Dóminum nostrum, qui concéptus est de Spíritu Sancto, natus ex María Vírgine, passus sub Póntio Piláto, crucifíxus, mórtuus, et sepúltus; descéndit ad ínfernos; tértia die resurréxit a mórtuis; ascéndit ad caelos, sedet ad déxteram Dei Patris omnipoténtis; inde ventúrus est iudicáre vivos et mórtuos. Credo in Spíritum Sanctum, sanctam Ecclésiam cathólicam, sanctórum communiónem, remissiónem peccatórum, carnis resurrectiónem, vitam aetérnam. Amen.

Eternal Father

Eternal Father, I offer you the Body and Blood, soul and divinity of your most beloved Son, our Lord Jesus Christ, in propitiation for our sins and those of the entire world.

For the Sake of His Sorrowful Passion

On account of his grievous suffering, have mercy on us and on the entire world.

Holy God

Holy God, Holy Mighty One, Holy Immortal One, have mercy on us and on the entire world.

PATER AETÉRNE

Pater aetérne, óffero tibi Corpus et Sánguinem, ánimam et divinitátem dilectíssimi Fílii tui, Dómini nostri Iesu Christi, in propitiatióne pro peccátis nostris et tótius mundi.

PRO DOLÓROSA

Pro dolorósa Eius passióne, miserére nobis et tótius mundi.

SANCTUS DEUS

Sanctus Deus, Sanctus Fortis, Sanctus Immortális, miserére nobis et tótius mundi.

More Marian Prayers

Hail, Holy Queen

(Prayed during Ordinary Time)

Hail Queen, Mother of mercy;
our life, sweetness, and hope, hail.
To you we cry, exiled children of Eve;
to you we sigh, groaning and weeping in this valley of tears.
Come, therefore, our Advocate,
turn those merciful eyes of yours toward us;
and show us Jesus, the blessed fruit of your womb, after this
      exile.
O merciful, O pious, O sweet Virgin Mary.
Amen.

Sweet Mother of the Redeemer

(Prayed during Advent)

Nourishing Mother of the Redeemer, you who remain our
      gate right through to heaven, and star of the sea,
come to the aid of the falling people who are working to rise:
you who gave life, while nature marveled, to your holy
      Life-Giver,
Virgin before and after, from the mouth of Gabriel taking up
      that "Hail," have mercy on sinners.
Amen.

Salve Regína

Salve Regína, Mater misericórdiae;
Vita, dulcédo, et spes nostra, salve.
Ad te clamámus éxsules fílii Evae;
Ad te suspirámus, geméntes et flentes in hac lacrimárum
    valle.
Eia ergo, Advocáta nostra,
Illos tuos misericórdes óculos ad nos convérte;
Et Iesum, benedíctum fructum ventris tui, nobis post hoc
    exsílium osténde.
O clemens, o pia, o dulcis Virgo María.
Amen.

Alma Redemptóris Mater

Alma Redemptóris Mater, quae pérvia caeli
    porta manes, et stella maris,
succúrre cadénti súrgere qui curat pópulo:
tu quae genuísti, natúra miránte, tuum sanctum
    Genitórem,
Virgo prius ac postérius, Gabriélis ab ore sumens
    illud Ave, peccatórum miserére.
Amen.

Hail, Queen of the Heavens

(Prayed during Lent)

Hail, Queen of the heavens,
Hail, Mistress of the Angels,
Welcome, root, welcome, gate,
from whom light has risen for the world:

Rejoice, glorious Virgin,
Splendid above all others,
Farewell, most fair one,
And on our behalf, prevail upon Christ.
Amen.

Queen of Heaven

(Prayed during the Easter season)

Queen of heaven, be glad, alleluia;
because he whom you deserved to bear, alleluia,
has risen, as he said, alleluia.
Pray for us to God, alleluia.
Let us pray.
God, through the resurrection of your Son, our Lord Jesus
Christ, you have given joy to the world; grant, we ask
you, that through his Bearer, the Virgin Mary, we may
obtain the joys of perpetual life.
Through Christ our Lord.
Amen.

AVE REGÍNA CAELÓRUM

Ave, Regína caelórum,
Ave, Dómina Angelórum:
Salve, radix, salve, porta
Ex qua mundo lux est orta:

Gaude, Virgo gloriósa,
Super omnes speciósa,
Vale, o valde decóra,
Et pro nobis Christum exóra.
Amen.

REGÍNA CAELI

Regína caeli, laetáre, allelúia;
Quia quem meruísti portáre, allelúia,
Resurréxit, sicut dixit, allelúia:
Ora pro nobis Deum, allelúia.
Orémus.
Deus, qui per resurrectiónem Fílii tui Dómini nostri
    Iesu Christi mundum laetificáre dignátus es, praesta,
    quaésumus, ut per eius Genetrícem Vírginem Maríam
    perpétuae capiámus gaúdia vitae.
Per Christum Dóminum nostrum.
Amen.

Under Your Protection

Under your protection we flee, holy Bearer of God.
Our supplications do not despise in our needs, but from all
dangers free us always, Virgin glorious and blessed.
Amen.

The Angel of the Lord

V. The angel of the Lord announced to Mary,
R. and she conceived from the Holy Spirit.

Hail Mary, full of grace, the Lord is with you. Blessed are you among women, and blessed the fruit of your womb, Jesus. Holy Mary, Mother of God, pray for us sinners, now and in the hour of our death. Amen.

V. Behold the maidservant of the Lord.
R. Let it be for me according to your word.

Hail Mary, full of grace, the Lord is with you. Blessed are you among women, and blessed the fruit of your womb, Jesus. Holy Mary, Mother of God, pray for us sinners, now and in the hour of our death. Amen.

V. And the Word was made flesh.
R. And has lived among us.

Sub Tuum Praesídium

Sub tuum praesídium confúgimus, sancta Dei Génetrix.
Nostras deprecatiónes ne despícias in necessitátibus, sed a
   perículis cunctis líbera nos semper, Virgo gloriósa et
   benedícta.
Amen.

Ángelus

V. Ángelus Dómini nuntiávit Maríae,
R. Et concépit de Spíritu Sancto.

Ave María, grátia plena, Dóminus tecum. Benedícta tu in
muliéribus, et benedíctus fructus ventris tui, Iesus. Sancta
María, Mater Dei, ora pro nobis peccatóribus, nunc et in
hora mortis nostrae. Amen.

V. Ecce ancílla Dómini.
R. Fiat mihi secúndum verbum tuum.

Ave María, grátia plena, Dóminus tecum. Benedícta tu in
muliéribus, et benedíctus fructus ventris tui, Iesus. Sancta
María, Mater Dei, ora pro nobis peccatóribus, nunc et in
hora mortis nostrae. Amen.

V. Et Verbum caro factum est.
R. Et habitávit in nobis.

Hail Mary, full of grace, the Lord is with you. Blessed are you among women, and blessed the fruit of your womb, Jesus. Holy Mary, Mother of God, pray for us sinners, now and in the hour of our death. Amen.

V. Pray for us, Holy Bearer of God,
R. So that we may be made worthy of the promises of Christ.

Let us pray.
We beg, Lord: fill our minds with your grace; so that we who have come to know the incarnation of Christ your Son by the Angel's announcement, through his suffering and cross may be led through to the glory of the resurrection. Through the same Christ our Lord. Amen.

Remember, O Most Gracious Virgin Mary

Remember, O most loving Virgin Mary,
that from the beginning it was never heard, that anyone running to your protection, imploring your help, begging your support, was left behind.
I, inspired by such confidence, run to you, Virgin of virgins, Mother, to you I come, in your presence, a groaning sinner I stand.
Do not, Mother of the Word, despise my words; but hear favorably and listen.
Amen.

Ave María, grátia plena, Dóminus tecum. Benedícta tu in muliéribus, et benedíctus fructus ventris tui, Iesus. Sancta María, Mater Dei, ora pro nobis peccatóribus, nunc et in hora mortis nostrae. Amen.

V. Ora pro nobis, Sancta Dei Génetrix.
R. *Ut digni efficiamur promissionibus Christi.*

Orémus.
Grátiam tuam, quaésumus,
Dómine, méntibus nostris infúnde;
ut qui, Ángelo nuntiánte,
Christi Fílii tui incarnatiónem cognóvimus,
per passiónem eius et crucem,
ad resurrectiónis glóriam perducámur.
Per eúndem Christum Dóminum nostrum. Amen.

MEMORÁRE

Memoráre, O piíssima Virgo María,
non esse audítum a saéculo, quemquam ad tua curréntem praesídia, tua implorántem auxília, tua peténtem suffrágia, esse derelíctum.
Ego tali animátus [*if female,* animáta] confidéntia, ad te, Virgo vírginum, Mater, curro, ad te vénio, coram te gemens peccátor assísto.
Noli, Mater Verbi, verba mea despícere; sed audi propítia et exaúdi.
Amen.

VARIOUS PRAYERS

Come, Holy Spirit, Fill

Come, Holy Spirit, fill the hearts of your faithful, and ignite in them the fire of your love.

V. Send out your Spirit and they will be created;
R. And you will renew the face of the earth.
Let us pray:

God, you who have taught the hearts of the faithful through the light of the Holy Spirit: grant us to discern what is right in the same Spirit, and always to rejoice in his consolation. Through Christ our Lord. Amen.

Nicene Creed

I believe in one God,
Father almighty,
Maker of heaven and earth,
of all that is visible and invisible,
And in one Lord Jesus Christ,
only-begotten Son of God
born of the Father
before all ages:
God from God, Light from Light,
true God from true God,
begotten, not made, consubstantial with the Father,
through him all was made;
who for the sake of humankind
and for the sake of our salvation,

VENI, SANCTE SPÍRITUS, REPLE

Veni, Sancte Spíritus, reple tuórum corda fidélium, et tui amóris in eis ignem accénde.

V. Emítte Spíritum tuum et creábuntur;
R. *Et renovábis fáciem terrae.*
Orémus:

Deus, qui corda fidélium Sancti Spíritus illustratióne docuísti: da nobis in éodem Spíritu recta sapére, et de eius semper consolatióne gaudére. Per Christum Dóminum nostrum. Amen.

SÝMBOLUM NICAÉNUM

Credo in unum Deum,
Patrem omnipoténtem,
Factórem caeli et terrae,
visibílium ómnium et invisibílium
Et in unum Dóminum Iesum Christum,
Fílium Dei unigénitum
et ex Patre natum
ante ómnia saécula:
Deum de Deo, Lumen de Lúmine,
Deum verum de Deo vero,
génitum, non factum, consubstantiálem Patri,
per quem ómnia facta sunt;
qui propter nos hómines
et propter nostram salútem,

descended from heaven,

and was incarnate of the Holy Spirit from the Virgin Mary
    and became human,

who also was crucified for us under Pontius Pilate,

suffered, and was buried,

and resurrected on the third day according to the Scriptures,

and ascended into heaven,

is seated at the right hand of the Father,

from thence he will come in glory,

to judge the living and the dead,

whose reign will never end.

And in the Holy Spirit,

Lord and lifegiver,

who proceeds from the Father and Son,

who with Father and Son alike is adored and glorified,

who spoke through the prophets.

And one holy catholic and apostolic Church.

I confess one Baptism for the remission of sins.

And I expect the resurrection of the dead,

and life in the age to come.

Amen.

descéndit de caelis,

et incarnátus est de Spíritu Sancto ex Maria Vírgine et homo
    factus est,

crucifíxus étiam pro nobis sub Póntio Piláto,

passus et sepúltus est,

et resurréxit tértia die secúndum Scriptúras,

et ascéndit in caelum,

sedet ad déxteram Patris,

et íterum ventúrus est cum glória,

iudicáre vivos et mórtuos,

cuius regni non erit finis.

Et in Spíritum Sanctum,

Dóminum et vivificántem,

qui ex Patre Filióque procédit,

qui cum Patre et Fílio simul adorátur et conglorificátur,

qui locútus est per prophétas.

Et unam sanctam cathólicam et apostólicam Ecclésiam.

Confíteor unum Baptísma in remissiónem peccatórum.

Et exspécto resurrectiónem mortuórum,

et vitam ventúri saéculi.

Amen.

ACT OF FAITH

Lord God, with a firm faith I believe and confess each and every thing that the holy Catholic Church teaches, because you, God, have revealed all these things, who are eternal truth and wisdom, who can neither deceive nor be deceived. In this faith, I resolve to live and to die. Amen.

ACT OF HOPE

Lord God, I hope through your grace to obtain the forgiveness of all my sins, and after this life to be in eternal happiness, because you have promised, who are infinitely powerful, faithful, kind, and merciful. In this hope, I resolve to live and to die. Amen.

ACT OF LOVE

Lord God, I love you above all things and my neighbor for your sake, because you are the greatest, infinite, and most perfect good, worthy of all my love. In this charity, I resolve to live and to die. Amen.

Actus Fidéi

Dómine Deus, firma fide credo et confíteor ómnia et síngula quae sancta ecclésia Cathólica propónit, quia tu, Deus, ea ómnia revelásti, qui es aetérna véritas et sapiéntia, quae nec fallére nec falli potest. In hac fide vivére et mori státuo. Amen.

Actus Spei

Dómine Deus, spero per grátiam tuam remissiónem ómnium peccatórum, et post hanc vitam aetérnam felicitátem me esse consecutúrum, quia tu promisísti, qui es infínite potens, fidélis, benígnus, et mísericors. In hac spe vivére et mori státuo. Amen.

Actus Caritátis

Dómine Deus, amo te super ómnia próximum meum propter te, quia tu es summum, infínitum, et perfectíssimum bonum, omni diléctione dignum. In hac caritáte vivére et mori státuo. Amen.

Take, Lord, Receive

Take, Lord, my entire liberty. Accept my memory, my intellect, and all my will. Whatever I have or possess you have lavished on me; I return it all to you, and I completely hand it over to the government of your will. May you give me only your love with your grace, and I am rich enough, nor do I ask for anything else beyond. Amen.

You Are God, We Praise You

You are God: we praise you.
You are Lord: we confess you.
You are the eternal Father: all the earth worships you.
To you all the angels, to you the heavens and all powers,
To you the cherubim and seraphim with unceasing voice cry
    out:
Holy, holy, holy, Lord God of Hosts.
Full are the heavens and earth of the majesty of your glory.
The glorious chorus of the apostles,
the praiseworthy company of the prophets;
the white-robed army of the martyrs praise you.
Through the whole world the holy Church confesses you:
Father of immense majesty;
Your Son, true, unique, worthy of worship;
as well as the Holy Spirit, the Paraclete.
You are king of glory, Christ.
You are the Son of the eternal Father.

SÚSCIPE

Súscipe, Dómine, univérsam meam libertátem. Áccipe memóriam, intelléctum, atque voluntátem omnem. Quidquid hábeo vel possídeo mihi lárgitus es; id tibi totum restítuo, ac tuae prorsus voluntáti trado gubernándum. Amórem tui solum cum grátia tua mihi dones, et dives sum satis, nec áliud quidquam ultra posco. Amen.

TE DEUM

Te Deum: laudámus.
Te Dóminum: confitémur.
Te aetérnum Patrem: omnis terra venerátur.
Tibi omnes ángeli, tibi caeli et univérsae potestátes,
Tibi chérubim et séraphim incessábili voce proclámant:

Sanctus, Sanctus, Sanctus, Dóminus Deus Sábaoth.
Pleni sunt caeli et terra maiestátis glóriae tuae.
Te gloriósus apostolórum chorus,
Te prophetárum laudábilis númerus,
Te mártyrum candidátus laudat exércitus.
Te per orbem terrárum sancta confitétur Ecclésia:
Patrem imménsae maiestátis;
Venerándum tuum verum et únicum Fílium;
Sanctum quoque Paráclitum Spíritum.
Tu rex glóriae, Christe.
Tu Patris sempitérnus es Fílius.

When you were about to take it upon yourself to liberate man, you did not abhor the Virgin's womb.

You, when the sting of death was conquered, opened the kingdom of heaven to believers.

You sit at the right hand of God, in the glory of the Father.

As judge you are believed to be coming.

Therefore we ask you, come to the aid of your servants, whom with your precious blood you have redeemed.

Make us to be numbered with your saints in eternal glory.

Make your people to be saved, Lord, and bless your inheritance.

And rule them, and raise them up to eternity.

Through each day we praise you.

And we praise your name into the age, and the age of the age.

Condescend, Lord, for this day to keep us without sin.

Have mercy on us, Lord, have mercy on us.

Let your mercy, Lord, be over us, just as we have hoped in you.

In you, Lord, I have hoped: let me not be confounded into eternity.

Amen.

Tu ad liberándum susceptúrus hóminem, non horruísti Vírginis úterum.

Tu, devícto mortis acúleo, aperuísti credéntibus regna caelórum.

Tu ad déxteram Dei sedes, in glória Patris.

Iudex créderis esse ventúrus.

Te ergo quaésumus, tuis fámulis súbveni, quos pretióso sánguine redemísti.

Aetérna fac cum sanctis tuis in glória numerári.

Salvum fac pópulum tuum, Dómine, et bénedic haereditáti tuae.

Et rege eos, et extólle illos usque in aetérnum.

Per síngulos dies benedícimus te.

Et laudámus nomen tuum in saéculum, et in saéculum saéculi.

Dignáre, Dómine, die isto sine peccáto nos custodíre.

Miserére nostri, Dómine, miserére nostri.

Fiat misericórdia tua, Dómine, super nos, quemádmodum sperávimus in te.

In te, Dómine, sperávi: non confúndar in aetérnum.

Amen.

Prayer to St. Michael

Holy Michael Archangel, defend us in the battle, against the wickedness and schemes of the devil be our protection. May God rebuke him, we humbly beg: and may, by the prince of heaven's army, Satan and all the other evil spirits who wander through the world seeking the loss of souls, by the power of God, be cast into hell. Amen.

May the Angels Lead You to Paradise

May the angels lead you into paradise; at your arrival, may the martyrs take you up, and lead you through into the holy city of Jerusalem. May the chorus of angels take you up, and with Lazarus, who once was poor, may you have eternal rest. Amen.

Eternal Rest

Rest eternal give him/her/them, Lord,
and may the perpetual light illuminate
    him/her/them.
May he/she/they rest in peace.
Amen.

Sancte Míchaël Archángele

Sancte Míchaël Archángele, defénde nos in proélio, contra nequítiam et insídias diáboli esto praesídium. Ímperet illi Deus, súpplices deprecámur: tuque, princeps milítiae caeléstis, Sátanam aliósque spíritus malígnos, qui ad perditiónem animárum pervagántur in mundo, divína virtúte, in inférnum detrúde. Amen.

In Paradísum

In paradísum dedúcant te ángeli; in tuo advéntu suscípiant te mártyres, et perdúcant te in civitátem sanctam Ierúsalem. Chorus angelórum te suscípiat, et cum Lázaro, quondam paúpere, aetérnam hábeas réquiem. Amen.

Réquiem Aetérnam

Réquiem aetérnam dona ei (*for more than one subject* eis), Dómine, et lux perpétua lúceat ei (*for more than one subject* eis).
Requiéscat (*for more than one subject* requiéscant) in pace. Amen.

WHERE CHARITY ABIDES

Where there is true charity (*or* Where there is charity and
   love),
God is there.
Love of Christ has gathered us together in one.
Let us rejoice, and in him take delight.
Let us fear and love the living God,
and with a sincere heart let us cherish one another.
Where there is true charity (*or* Where there is charity and
   love),
God is there.
Likewise, therefore, as we are gathered together in one,
let us beware not to be divided in mind.
Let ill-willed quarrels cease; let controversies cease;
and may Christ the God be in the midst of us.
Where there is true charity (*or* Where there is charity and
   love),
God is there.
Likewise also, may we with the blessed see
with elation your face, Christ, God:
a joy that is immense, and also virtuous.
Through the infinite ages of ages.
Amen.

UBI CÁRITAS

Ubi cáritas est vera (Ubi caritas et amor),

Deus ibi est.
Congregávit nos in unum Christi amor.
Exsultémus, et in ipso iucundémur.
Timeámus et amémus Deum vivum,
Et ex corde diligámus nos sincéro.
Ubi cáritas est vera (Ubi caritas et amor),

Deus ibi est.
Simul ergo cum in unum congregámur,
Ne nos mente dividámur, caveámus.
Cessent iúrgia malígna; cessent lites;
Et in médio nostri sit Christus Deus.
Ubi cáritas est vera (Ubi caritas et amor),

Deus ibi est.
Simul quoque cum beátis videámus,
Gloriánter vultum tuum, Christe Deus:
Gaúdium quod est imménsum, atque probum.
Saécula per infiníta saeculórum.
Amen.

LITANY OF THE HOLY SPIRIT

Lord, have mercy. *Lord, have mercy.*
Christ, have mercy. *Christ, have mercy.*
Lord, have mercy. *Lord, have mercy.*
Holy Spirit, proceeding from the Father and the Son,
Have mercy on us.
Spirit of the Lord, God of Israel,
Have mercy on us.
Ruler of men,
Have mercy on us.
Filling the world,
Have mercy on us.
Having all virtue,
Have mercy on us.
Engaged in all good things, and taking care of all things,
Have mercy on us.
Adorning the heavens, stable and secure,
Have mercy on us.
Spirit of truth, providing and distributing all things,
Have mercy on us.
Spirit of wisdom and understanding,
Have mercy on us.
Spirit of counsel, strength, knowledge, and piety,
Have mercy on us.
Spirit of the fear of the Lord and of prudence,
Have mercy on us.
Spirit, by whose inspiration God's holy men spoke,
Have mercy on us.

LITÁNIAE DE SANCTO SPÍRITU

Kýrie, eléison. *Kýrie, eléison.*
Christe, eléison. *Christe, eléison.*
Kýrie, eléison. *Kýrie, eléison.*
Spíritus sancte, a Patre Filióque procédens,
Miserére nobis.
Spíritus Dómini, Deus Ísrael,
Miserére nobis.
Dominátor hóminum,
Miserére nobis.
Replens orbem terrárum,
Miserére nobis.
Habens omnem virtútem,
Miserére nobis.
Ómnia bona óperans, et ómnia prospíciens,
Miserére nobis.
Ornans caelos, stábilis et secúrus,
Miserére nobis.
Spíritus veritátis, ómnia súggerens et distríbuens,
Miserére nobis.
Spíritus sapiéntiae et intelléctus,
Miserére nobis.
Spíritus consílii, fortitúdinis, sciéntiae, et pietátis,
Miserére nobis.
Spíritus timóris Dómini et prudéntiae,
Miserére nobis.
Spíritus, quo inspiránte locúti sunt sancti Dei hómines,
Miserére nobis.

You who are the proclaimer of things to come,
Have mercy on us.
The gift and promise of the Father,
Have mercy on us.
Holy Spirit, Paraclete, accusing the world,
Have mercy on us.
Spirit, by whom demons are thrown out,
Have mercy on us.
Spirit, from whom we are reborn,
Have mercy on us.
Spirit, through whom the love of God is diffused in our
hearts,
Have mercy on us.
Spirit of adoption of the sons of God,
Have mercy on us.
Spirit of grace and mercy,
Have mercy on us.
Spirit supporting our infirmity and restoring witness to our
spirit, that we are sons of God,
Have mercy on us.
Soft Spirit, kind, sweet above honey,
Have mercy on us.
Spirit, the pledge of our inheritance, leading us into the
righteous land,
Have mercy on us.
Original Spirit, life-giving and comforting,
Have mercy on us.
Spirit of salvation, judgment, and joy,
Have mercy on us.

Quae ventúra annúntians,
Miserére nobis.
Donum et promíssio Patris,
Miserére nobis.
Spíritus sancte, Paraclíte, árguens mundum,
Miserére nobis.
Spíritus, in quo daemónia eiiciúntur,
Miserére nobis.
Spíritus, ex quo renáscimur,
Miserére nobis.
Spíritus, per quem cáritas Dei diffúsa est
    in córdibus nostris,
Miserére nobis.
Spíritus adoptiónis filiórum Dei,
Miserére nobis.
Spíritus grátiae et misericórdiae,
Miserére nobis.
Spíritus ádiuvans infirmitátem nostram et reddens tes-
    timónium spirítui nostro, quod simus fílii Dei,
Miserére nobis.
Spíritus suavis, benígne, super mel dulcis,
Miserére nobis.
Spíritus, pignus hereditátis nostrae, dedúcens nos in terram
    rectam,
Miserére nobis.
Spíritus principális, vivíficans et confórtans,
Miserére nobis.
Spíritus salútis, iudícii, et gaúdii,
Miserére nobis.

Spirit of faith, peace, and eagerness,
Have mercy on us.
Spirit of humility, charity, and chastity,
Have mercy on us.
Spirit of kindness, goodness, forbearance,
    and gentleness,
Have mercy on us.
Spirit of mildness, truth, unity, and consolation,
Have mercy on us.
Spirit of compunction, promise, renewal,
    and sanctification,
Have mercy on us.
Spirit of life, patience, continence, and modesty,
Have mercy on us.
Spirit of all graces,
Have mercy on us.
Be gracious,
Spare us, holy Spirit.
Be gracious,
Listen to us, holy Spirit.
From the spirit of error,
Free us, Spirit of the living God.
From an impure spirit,
Free us, Spirit of the living God.
From the spirit of blasphemy,
Free us, Spirit of the living God.
From all stubbornness and despair,
Free us, Spirit of the living God.
From all presumption and contradiction of the truth,
Free us, Spirit of the living God.

Spíritus fidéi, pacis, et ardóris,
Miserére nobis.
Spíritus humilitátis, caritátis, et castitátis,
Miserére nobis.
Spíritus benignitátis, bonitátis, longanimitátis, ac
    mansuetúdinis,
Miserére nobis.
Spíritus lenitátis, veritátis, unitátis ac consolatiónis,
Miserére nobis.
Spíritus compunctiónis, promissiónis, renovatiónis, ac
    sanctificatiónis,
Miserére nobis.
Spíritus vitae, patiéntiae, continéntiae, ac modéstiae,
Miserére nobis.
Spíritus ómnium gratiárum,
Miserére nobis.
Propítius esto,
Parce nobis, sancte Spíritus.
Propitius esto,
Exaúdi nos, sancte Spíritus.
A spíritu erróris,
Líbera nos, Spíritus Dei vivi.
A spíritu immúndo,
Líbera nos, Spíritus Dei vivi.
A spíritu blasphémiae,
Líbera nos, Spíritus Dei vivi.
Ab omni obstinatióne et desperatióne,
Líbera nos, Spíritus Dei vivi.
Ab omni praesumptióne et veritátis contradictióne,
Líbera nos, Spíritus Dei vivi.

From all malice and every vicious habit,
Free us, Spirit of the living God.
From envy of brotherly love,
Free us, Spirit of the living God.
From final impenitence,
Free us, Spirit of the living God.
Through your eternal procession from the Father and the Son,
Free us, Spirit of the living God.
Through your invisible anointing,
Free us, Spirit of the living God.
Through all the fullness of grace by which you have always
possessed the Virgin Mary,
Free us, Spirit of the living God.
Through the overflowing depth of holiness by which you
made the Mother of God teem with the conception of
the Word,
Free us, Spirit of the living God.
Through your holy appearance in the baptism of Christ,
Free us, Spirit of the living God.
Through your saving coming upon the apostles,
Free us, Spirit of the living God.
Through your unspeakable goodness, by which you govern
the Church, counsel the leaders, strengthen the martyrs,
enlighten the teachers, and institute religious houses,
Free us, Spirit of the living God.
We sinners,
We ask you, hear us.
That in the spirit we may walk, and the desires of the flesh
we may not fulfill,
We ask you, hear us.

Ab omni malítia et prava consuetúdine,
Líbera nos, Spíritus Dei vivi.
Ab invídia fratérnae caritátis,
Líbera nos, Spíritus Dei vivi.
A fináli impaeniténtia,
Líbera nos, Spíritus Dei vivi.
Per aetérnam a Patre et Filio processiónem tuam,
Líbera nos, Spíritus Dei vivi.
Per invisíbilem unctiónem tuam,
Líbera nos, Spíritus Dei vivi.
Per omnem gratiárum plenitúdinem qua Vírginem Maríam
semper possedísti,
Líbera nos, Spíritus Dei vivi.
Per supereffluéntem sanctitátis abýssum qua conceptióne
Verbi Matrem Dei inundáre fecísti,

Líbera nos, Spíritus Dei vivi.
Per sanctam in baptísmo Christi apparitiónem tuam,
Líbera nos, Spíritus Dei vivi.
Per salutárem super apóstolos advéntum tuum,
Líbera nos, Spíritus Dei vivi.
Per ineffábilem bonitátem tuam, qua Ecclésiam gubérnas,
concílias praesides, mártyres corróboras, doctóres
illúminas, religiónes instítuis,
Líbera nos, Spíritus Dei vivi.
Peccatóres,
Te rogámus, audi nos.
Ut in spíritu ambulémus, et desidéria carnis non
adimpleámus,
Te rogámus, audi nos.

That we may never grieve you,
We ask you, hear us.
That you would condescend to keep all Ecclesiastical Orders in the holy religion, and in the true spirit,
We ask you, hear us.
That you would condescend to give the whole Christian people one heart and one soul,
We ask you, hear us.
That you would condescend to give us the fullness of all the virtues,
We ask you, hear us.
That you would deem worthy to hear us.
We ask you, hear us.
Spirit of God,
We ask you, hear us.
Lamb of God, who takes away the sins of the world,
Pour into us your Holy Spirit.
Lamb of God, who takes away the sins of the world,
Send into us the promised Spirit of the Father.
Lamb of God, who takes away the sins of the world,
Give us a good spirit.
The Spirit of the Lord has filled the world:
And this Spirit, which contains all things, has knowledge of speech.
Let us pray.

Ut Te numquam contristémus,

Te rogámus, audi nos.

Ut omnes Ecclesiásticos Órdines in sancta religióne, et vero spíritu conserváre dígneris,

Te rogámus, audi nos.

Ut cuncto pópulo Christiáno cor unum et ánimam unam donáre dígneris,

Te rogámus, audi nos.

Ut virtútum ómnium compleméntum nobis donáre dígneris,

Te rogámus, audi nos.

Ut nos exaudíre dígneris,

Te rogámus, audi nos.

Spíritus Dei,

Te rogámus, audi nos.

Agnus Dei, qui tollis peccáta mundi,

Effúnde in nos Sanctum Spíritum.

Agnus Dei, qui tollis peccáta mundi,

Emítte in nos promíssum Patris Spíritum.

Agnus Dei, qui tollis peccáta mundi,

Da nobis spíritum bonum.

Spíritus Dómini replévit orbem terrárum:

Et hoc, quod cóntinet ómnia, sciéntiam habet vocis.

Orémus.

We beg you, Lord, let the strength of your Holy Spirit be with us, which both mercifully cleans our hearts, and keeps us safe from all opposition. Through our Lord Jesus Christ your Son, who with you lives and reigns in the unity of the same Holy Spirit, God, through all the ages of ages. Amen.

Litany of the Saints

Lord, have mercy. *Lord, have mercy.*
Christ, have mercy. *Christ, have mercy.*
Lord, have mercy. *Lord, have mercy.*
Christ, hear us. *Christ, hear us.*
Christ, listen to us. *Christ, listen to us.*
God, the Father of heaven,
Have mercy on us.
God, the Son, Redeemer of the world,
Have mercy on us.
God, the Holy Spirit,
Have mercy on us.
Holy Trinity, one God,
Have mercy on us.
Holy Mary,
Pray for us.
Holy Bearer of God,
Pray for us.
Holy Virgin of virgins,
Pray for us.

Adsit nobis, quaésumus Dómine, virtus Spíritus Sancti, quae et corda nostra cleménter expúrget, et ab ómnibus tueátur advérsis. Per Dóminum nostrum Iesum Christum fílium tuum, qui tecum vivit et regnat in unitáte eiúsdem Spíritus Sancti, Deus, per ómnia saécula saeculórum. Amen.

LITÁNIAE SANCTÓRUM

Kýrie, eléison. *Kýrie, eléison.*
Christe, eléison. *Christe, eléison.*
Kýrie, eléison. *Kýrie, eléison.*
Christe, audi nos. *Christe, audi nos.*
Christe, exaúdi nos. *Christe, exaúdi nos.*
Pater de caelis, Deus,
Miserére nobis.
Fili, Redémptor mundi, Deus,
Miserére nobis.
Spíritus Sancte, Deus,
Miserére nobis.
Sancta Trínitas, unus Deus,
Miserére nobis.
Sancta María,
Ora pro nobis.
Sancta Dei Génetrix,
Ora pro nobis.
Sancta Virgo vírginum,
Ora pro nobis.

Saint Michael,
Pray for us.
Saint Gabriel,
Pray for us.
Saint Raphael,
Pray for us.
All holy Angels and Archangels,
Pray for us.
All holy blessed orders of Spirits,
Pray for us.
Saint John the Baptist,
Pray for us.
Saint Joseph,
Pray for us.
All holy Patriarchs and Prophets,
Pray for us.
Saint Peter,
Pray for us.
Saint Paul,
Pray for us.
Saint Andrew,
Pray for us.
Saint James,
Pray for us.
Saint John,
Pray for us.
Saint Thomas,
Pray for us.
Saint James,
Pray for us.

Sancte Michaël,
Ora pro nobis.
Sancte Gábriel,
Ora pro nobis.
Sancte Ráphael,
Ora pro nobis.
Omnes sancti Ángeli et Archángeli,
Oráte pro nobis.
Omnes sancti beatórum Spirítuum órdines,
Oráte pro nobis.
Sancte Ioánnes Baptísta,
Ora pro nobis.
Sancte Ioseph,
Ora pro nobis.
Omnes sancti Patriárchae et Prophétae,
Orate pro nobis.
Sancte Petre,
Ora pro nobis.
Sancte Paule,
Ora pro nobis.
Sancte Ándrea,
Ora pro nobis.
Sancte Iácobe,
Ora pro nobis.
Sancte Ioánnes,
Ora pro nobis.
Sancte Thoma,
Ora pro nobis.
Sancte Iácobe,
Ora pro nobis.

Saint Philip,
Pray for us.
Saint Bartholomew,
Pray for us.
Saint Matthew,
Pray for us.
Saint Simon,
Pray for us.
Saint Thaddeus,
Pray for us.
Saint Matthias,
Pray for us.
Saint Barnabas,
Pray for us.
Saint Luke,
Pray for us.
Saint Mark,
Pray for us.
All holy Apostles and Evangelists,
Pray for us.
All holy disciples of the Lord,
Pray for us.
All the holy Innocents,
Pray for us.
Saint Stephen,
Pray for us.
Saint Laurence,
Pray for us.
Saint Vincent,
Pray for us.

Sancte Philíppe,
Ora pro nobis.
Sancte Bartolómaee,
Ora pro nobis.
Sancte Mátthaee,
Ora pro nobis.
Sancte Simon,
Ora pro nobis.
Sancte Tháddaee,
Ora pro nobis.
Sancte Matthía,
Ora pro nobis.
Sancte Bárnaba,
Ora pro nobis.
Sancte Luca,
Ora pro nobis.
Sancte Marce,
Ora pro nobis.
Omnes sancti Apóstoli et Evangelístae,
Oráte pro nobis.
Omnes sancti discípuli Dómini,
Oráte pro nobis.
Omnes sancti Innocéntes,
Oráte pro nobis.
Sancte Stéphane,
Ora pro nobis.
Sancte Laurénti,
Ora pro nobis.
Sancte Vincénti,
Ora pro nobis.

Saints Fabian and Sebastian,
Pray for us.
Saints John and Paul,
Pray for us.
Saints Cosmas and Damian,
Pray for us.
Saints Gervase and Protase,
Pray for us.
All holy martyrs,
Pray for us.
Saint Sylvester,
Pray for us.
Saint Gregory,
Pray for us.
Saint Ambrose,
Pray for us.
Saint Augustine,
Pray for us.
Saint Jerome,
Pray for us.
Saint Martin,
Pray for us.
Saint Nicholas,
Pray for us.
All holy Pontiffs and Confessors,
Pray for us.
All holy Doctors,
Pray for us.
Saint Anthony,
Pray for us.

Sancti Fabiáne et Sebastiáne,
Orate pro nobis.
Sancti Iohánnes et Paule,
Oráte pro nobis.
Sancti Cosma et Damiáne,
Oráte pro nobis.
Sancti Gervási et Protási,
Oráte pro nobis.
Omnes sancti mártyres,
Oráte pro nobis.
Sancte Sylvéster,
Ora pro nobis.
Sancte Gregóri,
Ora pro nobis.
Sancte Ambrósi,
Ora pro nobis.
Sancte Augustíne,
Ora pro nobis.
Sancte Hierónyme,
Ora pro nobis.
Sancte Martíne,
Ora pro nobis.
Sancte Nicólaë,
Ora pro nobis.
Omnes sancti Pontífices et Confessóres,
Oráte pro nobis.
Omnes sancti Doctóres,
Oráte pro nobis.
Sancte Ántoni,
Ora pro nobis.

Saint Benedict,
Pray for us.
Saint Bernard,
Pray for us.
Saint Dominic,
Pray for us.
Saint Francis,
Pray for us.
All holy Priests and Levites,
Pray for us.
All holy Monks and Hermits,
Pray for us.
Saint Mary Magdalene,
Pray for us.
Saint Agatha,
Pray for us.
Saint Lucy,
Pray for us.
Saint Agnes,
Pray for us.
Saint Cecilia,
Pray for us.
Saint Catharine,
Pray for us.
Saint Anastasia,
Pray for us.
All holy Virgins and Widows,
Pray for us.
All Holy Men and Women of God,
Intercede for us.

Sancte Benedícte,
Ora pro nobis.
Sancte Bernárde,
Ora pro nobis.
Sancte Domínice,
Ora pro nobis.
Sancte Francísce,
Ora pro nobis.
Omnes sancti Sacerdótes et Lévitae,
Oráte pro nobis.
Omnes sancti Mónachi et Eremítae,
Oráte pro nobis.
Sancta María Magdaléna,
Ora pro nobis.
Sancta Ágatha,
Ora pro nobis.
Sancta Lucía,
Ora pro nobis.
Sancta Agnes,
Ora pro nobis.
Sancta Caecília,
Ora pro nobis.
Sancta Catharína,
Ora pro nobis.
Sancta Anastásia,
Ora pro nobis.
Omnes sanctae Vírgines et Víduae,
Oráte pro nobis.
Omnes Sancti et Sanctae Dei,
Intercédite pro nobis.

Be favorable,
Spare us, Lord.
Be favorable,
Listen to us, Lord.
From all evil,
Free us, Lord.
From all sin,
Free us, Lord.
From your wrath,
Free us, Lord.
From sudden and unforeseen death,
Free us, Lord.
From the schemes of the devil,
Free us, Lord.
From wrath and hatred and all ill will,
Free us, Lord.
From a spirit of fornication,
Free us, Lord.
From lightning and tempest,
Free us, Lord.
From the scourge of earthquake,
Free us, Lord.
From plague, famine, and war,
Free us, Lord.
From perpetual death,
Free us, Lord.
Through the mystery of your holy Incarnation,
Free us, Lord.
Through your coming,
Free us, Lord.

Propítius esto,
Parce nos, Dómine.
Propítius esto,
Exaúdi nos, Dómine.
Ab omni malo,
Líbera nos, Dómine.
Ab omni peccáto,
Líbera nos, Dómine.
Ab ira tua,
Líbera nos, Dómine.
A subitánea et improvísa morte,
Líbera nos, Dómine.
Ab insídiis diáboli,
Líbera nos, Dómine.
Ab ira et odio et omni mala voluntáte,
Líbera nos, Dómine.
A spíritu fornicatiónis,
Líbera nos, Dómine.
A fúlgure et tempestáte,
Líbera nos, Dómine.
A flagéllo terraemótus,
Líbera nos, Dómine.
A peste, fame et bello,
Líbera nos, Dómine.
A morte perpétua,
Líbera nos, Dómine.
Per mystérium sanctae Incarnatiónis tuae,
Líbera nos, Dómine.
Per advéntum tuum,
Líbera nos, Dómine.

Through your nativity,
Free us, Lord.
Through your baptism and holy youth,
Free us, Lord.
Through your cross and suffering,
Free us, Lord.
Through your death and tomb,
Free us, Lord.
Through your holy resurrection,
Free us, Lord.
Through your wonderful ascension,
Free us, Lord.
Through the coming of the Holy Spirit,
Free us, Lord.
In the day of judgment,
Free us, Lord.
We sinners,
We ask you, hear us.
That you may spare us,
We ask you, hear us.
That you may be patient with us,
We ask you, hear us.
That you may condescend to lead us through to true
    repentance,
We ask you, hear us.
That you may condescend to rule and preserve your Church,
We ask you, hear us.
That you may condescend to preserve the Apostolic house
    and all ecclesiastical orders in the holy faith,
We ask you, hear us.

Per nativitátem tuam,
Líbera nos, Dómine.
Per baptísmum et sanctum ieiúnium tuum,
Líbera nos, Dómine.
Per crucem et passiónem tuam,
Líbera nos, Dómine.
Per mortem et sepultúram tuam,
Líbera nos, Dómine.
Per sanctam resurrectiónem tuam,
Líbera nos, Dómine.
Per admirábilem ascensiónem tuam,
Líbera nos, Dómine.
Per advéntum Spíritus Sancti Paraclíti,
Líbera nos, Dómine.
In die iudícii,
Líbera nos, Dómine.
Peccatóres,
Te rogámus, audi nos.
Ut nobis parcas,
Te rogámus, audi nos.
Ut nobis indúlgeas,
Te rogámus, audi nos.
Ut ad veram paeniténtiam nos perdúcere
    dígneris,
Te rogámus, audi nos.
Ut Ecclésiam tuam sanctam régere et conserváre dígneris,
Te rogámus, audi nos.
Ut domum Apostólicum et omnes ecclesiásticos órdines in
    sancta religióne conserváre dígneris,
Te rogámus, audi nos.

That you may condescend to humble the enemies of the holy Church,

We ask you, hear us.

That to Christian kings and princes you may condescend to give peace and true concord,

We ask you, hear us.

That on the whole Christian people you may condescend to lavish peace and unity,

We ask you, hear us.

That you may condescend to call all the straying back to the unity of the Church, and lead all unbelievers to the light of the Gospel,

We ask you, hear us.

That you would condescend to comfort and preserve us ourselves in your service,

We ask you, hear us.

That you would lift up our minds to heavenly things,

We ask you, hear us.

That you would reward all our benefactors with eternal goods,

We ask you, hear us.

That you would snatch away from eternal damnation our souls and those of our brothers, relations, and benefactors,

We ask you, hear us.

That you would condescend to give and preserve the fruits of the earth,

We ask you, hear us.

Ut inímicos sanctae Ecclésiae humiliáre
  dígneris,
Te rogámus, audi nos.
Ut régibus et princípibus Christiánis pacem et veram
  concórdiam donáre dígneris,
Te rogámus, audi nos.
Ut cuncto pópulo Christiáno pacem et unitátem largíri
  dígneris,
Te rogámus, audi nos.
Ut omnes errántes ad unitátem Ecclésiae revocáre,
  et infidéles univérsos ad Evangélii lumen perdúcere
  dígneris,
Te rogámus, audi nos.
Ut nosmetípsos in tuo sancto servítio confortáre et conserváre
  dígneris,
Te rogámus, audi nos.
Ut mentes nostras ad caeléstia desidéria érigas,
Te rogámus, audi nos.
Ut ómnibus benefactóribus nostris sempitérna bona
  retríbuas,
Te rogámus, audi nos.
Ut ánimas nostras, fratrum, propinquórum et benefactórum
  nostrórum ab aetérna damnatióne erípias,
Te rogámus, audi nos.
Ut fructus terrae dare et conserváre
  dígneris,
Te rogámus, audi nos.

That to all the faithful departed you would deem worthy to
give eternal rest,
We ask you, hear us.
That you would deem worthy to hear us,
We ask you, hear us.
Son of God,
We ask you, hear us.
Lamb of God, you who take away the sins of the world,
Spare us, Lord.
Lamb of God, you who take away the sins of the world,
Hear us, Lord.
Lamb of God, you who take away the sins of the world,
Have mercy on us.
Christ, hear us.
Christ, listen to us.
Lord, have mercy. *Lord, have mercy.*
Christ, have mercy. *Christ, have mercy.*
Lord, have mercy. *Lord, have mercy.*

Ut ómnibus fidélibus defúnctis réquiem aetérnam donáre dígneris,

Te rogámus, audi nos.

Ut nos exaudíre dígneris,

Te rogámus, audi nos.

Fili Dei,

Te rogámus, audi nos.

Agnus Dei, qui tollis peccáta mundi,

Parce nobis, Domine.

Agnus Dei, qui tollis peccáta mundi,

Exaúdi nos, Domine.

Agnus Dei, qui tollis peccáta mundi,

Miserere nobis.

Christe, audi nos.

Christe, exaúdi nos.

Kýrie, eléison. *Kýrie, eléison.*

Christe, eléison. *Christe, eléison.*

Kýrie, eléison. *Kýrie, eléison.*

GOSPEL SEQUENCES

Christians, to the Paschal Victim

(Gospel Sequence for Easter Sunday)

Praises to the paschal victim
let Christians offer.
The Lamb has redeemed the sheep:
the innocent Christ
has reconciled sinners to the Father.
Death and life have
contended in wondrous combat:
the leader of life, once dead,
reigns living.
Tell us, Mary,
what have you seen along the way?
"I saw the tomb of the living Christ,
and the glory of his rising.
I saw Angels attesting,
and the napkin and graveclothes.
Christ, my hope, has risen:
he will go before his own into Galilee."
We know that Christ has risen
truly from the dead;
you, victorious King, have mercy on us.
Amen. Alleluia.

Víctimae Pascháli Laudes

Víctimae pascháli laudes
ímmolent Christiani.
Agnus redémit oves:
Christus ínnocens Patri
reconciliávit peccatóres.
Mors et vita duéllo
conflixére mirándo:
dux vitae, mórtuus,
regnat vivus.
Dic nobis, Maria,
quid vidísti in via?
"Sepúlcrum Christi vivéntis,
et glóriam vidi resurgéntis.
Angélicos testes,
sudárium, et vestes.
Surréxit Christus spes mea:
praecédet suos in Galilaéam."
Scimus Christum surrexísse
a mórtuis vere;
tu nobis, victor Rex, miserére.
Amen. Allelúia.

Come, Holy Spirit

(Gospel Sequence for Pentecost Sunday)

Come, Holy Spirit,
and send the heavenly radiance of your light.
Come, father of the poor,
come, giver of gifts,
come, light of hearts.
Greatest comforter,
sweet guest of the soul,
sweet refreshment.
In labor, rest,
in heat, temperance,
in tears, solace.
O most blessed light,
fill the innermost heart
of your faithful.
Without your power
there is nothing in humankind,
nothing that is not harmful.
Cleanse what is stained,
water what is dry,
heal what is wounded.
Bend what is rigid,
warm the chill,
correct what goes astray.
Give to your faithful,
to those who trust in you,
the sevenfold gifts.

VENI, SANCTE SPÍRITUS

Veni, Sancte Spíritus,
et emítte caelitus lucis tuae rádium.
Veni, pater paúperum,
veni, dator múnerum,
veni, lumen córdium.
Consolátor óptime,
dulcis hospes ánimae,
dulce refrigérium.
In labóre réquies,
in aestu tempéries,
in fletu solácium.
O lux beatíssima,
reple cordis íntima
tuórum fidélium.
Sine tuo númine,
nihil est in hómine,
nihil est innóxium.
Lava quod est sórdidum,
riga quod est áridum,
sana quod est saúcium.
Flecte quod est rígidum,
fove quod est frígidum,
rege quod est dévium.
Da tuis fidélibus,
in te confidéntibus,
sacrum septenárium.

Grant the reward of virtue,
grant salvation,
grant unending joy.
Amen.

Praise, O Zion

(Gospel Sequence for Corpus Christi)

Praise, O Zion, your Savior,
Praise your leader and shepherd
in hymns and songs.
Praise him as much as you are able,
for he is beyond all praises and you will never praise him
    sufficiently.
A special theme of praise—
the Bread living and life-giving—
is put before us today:
At the table during the Holy Supper,
it was given to the twelve
without any ambiguity.
Therefore, let praise be full, let it resound.
Delightful and beautiful be
the rejoicing of our minds.
For this is the solemn day
to commemorate this table's first
institution.
At this table of the new king,
the new passover of the new law
puts an end to the older rite.

Da virtútis méritum,
da salútis éxitum,
da perénne gaúdium.
Amen.

LAUDA, SION

Lauda, Sion salvatórem,
Lauda ducem et pastórem
In hymnis et cánticis.
Quantum potes tantum au de,
Quia maior omni laude
Nec laudáre súfficis.
Laudis thema speciális—
Panis vivus et vitális—
Hódie propónitur:
Quem in sacrae mensa coenae
Turbae fratrum duodénae
Datum non ambígitur.
Sit laus plena, sit sonóra.
Sit iucúnda, sit decóra
Mentis iubilátio.
Dies enim solémnis ágitur
In qua mensae prima recólitur
Huius institútio.
In hac mensa novi regis,
Novum pascha novae legis
Phase vetus términat.

The new replaces the old;
shadow is dispelled by truth;
night is eliminated by light.
Christ wanted what he did at supper
to be repeated
in his memory.
In accord with his holy instruction,
bread and wine
we consecrate as salvation's victim.
By faith Christians believe
that bread is changed into flesh
and wine into blood.
This cannot be understood or seen,
but living faith affirms
that things outside order take place.
Under the different species,
which are now signs and not things,
lie hidden wonders.
His body is food, his blood is drink,
yet Christ remains whole
under each species.
Not severed,
not broken, not divided:
the whole Christ is received.
Whether one or a thousand,
they receive the same,
And Christ is not diminished by being consumed.
The good and the evil alike receive,
but with different effects,
life or death.

Vetustátem nóvitas;
Umbram fugat véritas;
Noctem lux elíminat.
Quod in coena Christus gessit
Faciéndum hoc expréssit
In sui memóriam.
Docti sacris institútis,
Panem vinum in salútis
Consecrámus hóstiam.
Dogma datur Christiánis
Quod in carnem transit panis
Et vinum in sánguinem.
Quod non capis, quod non vides,
Animósa firm at fides
Praeter rerum órdinem.
Sub divérsis speciébus,
Signis tantum et non rebus,
Latent res exímiae.
Caro cibus, sanguis potus,
Manet tamen Christus totus
Sub utráque spécie.
A suménte non concísus,
Non confráctus, non divísus:
Integer accípitur.
Sumit unus, sumunt mille,
Quantum isti, tantum ille,
Nec sumptus consúmitur.
Sumunt boni, sumunt mali,
Sorte tamen inaequáli,
Vitae vel intéritus.

Death to evil ones, life to the good—
see how receiving the same thing
produces different results.
If the sacrament is broken,
have no doubt and remember
that there is as much in a fragment
as in the whole.
There is no division of the reality:
only the sign is fractured;
neither does breaking lessen the state or size
of the One hidden under the sign.
Behold the bread of angels
has become food for those on the way,
truly bread for sons,
not to be thrown to dogs.
It was prefigured in type:
when Isaac was brought as a sacrifice,
when a lamb was chosen for Passover,
when manna was given to the fathers.
Good shepherd, true bread,
Jesus, have mercy on us.
You, feed us and protect us.
You, grant that we see goodness
in the land of the living.
You, who know and can do everything,
who feeds us here on earth:
Make us your guests,
coheirs and companions
of the holy citizens.
Amen. Alleluia.

Mors est malis, vita bonis—
Vide paris sumptiónis
Quam sit dis par éxitus.
Fracto demum sacraménto,
Ne vacíles sed meménto
Tantum esse sub fragménto
Quantum toto tégitur.
Nulla rei fit scissúra:
Signi tantum fit fractúra;
Qua nec status nec statúra
Signáti minúitur.
Ecce panis angelórum
Factus cibus viatórum,
Vere panis filiórum,
Non mitténdus cánibus.
In figúris praesignátur:
Cum Isaac immolátur,
Agnus Paschae deputátur,
Datur manna pátribus.
Bone pastor, panis vere,
Iesu, nostri miserére.
Tu, nos pasce, nos tuére,
Tu, nos bona fac vidére
In terra vivéntium.
Tu, qui cuncta scis et vales,
Qui nos pascis hie mortáles:
Tuos ibi commensáles,
Coherédes et sodáles
Fac sanctórum cívium.
Amen. Allelúia.

At the Cross Her Station Keeping

(Gospel Sequence for Our Lady of Sorrows)

The sorrowful mother stood
weeping beside the Cross
on which her Son was hanging.
Through her groaning soul,
grieving and sorrowful,
a sword passed.
O how sad and afflicted
was that blessed
mother of the Only-Begotten!
Who mourned and was sorrowful,
the pious Mother, looking
at the incomparable torment of her child.
What person would not weep
seeing the Mother of Christ
in such agony?
Who would not be able to feel compassion
contemplating Christ's Mother
suffering with her Son?
For the sins of his people
she saw Jesus in torment
and subjected to scourging.
She saw her sweet Child
dying in desolation
while he gave up his spirit.
O Mother, font of love,
make me feel your sorrow

STABAT MATER

Stabat mater dolorósa
iuxta Crucem lacrimósa
dum pendébat Fílius.
Cuius ánimam geméntem,
contristátam et doléntem,
pertransívit gládius.
O quam tristis et afflícta
fuit illa benedícta
mater Unigéniti!
Quae moerébat et dolébat,
pia Mater, dum vidébat
nati poenas ínclyti.
Quis est homo qui non fleret
matrem Christi si vidéret
in tanto supplício?
Quis non posset contristári
Christi Matrem contemplári
doléntem cum Fílio?
Pro peccátis suae gentis
vidit Iésum in torméntis
et flagéllis súbditum.
Vidit suum dulcem Natum
moriéndo desolátum
dum emísit spíritum.
Eia, Mater, fons amóris,
me sentíre vim dolóris

so that I may grieve with you.
Make my heart burn
in the love of Christ God
so that I may please him.
Holy Mother, grant that each wound
of the crucified is driven
into my heart.
That of your wounded child,
who suffered for me,
I may share the pain.
Make me sincerely weep with you,
lament the crucified,
while I live.
To stand beside the Cross with you
and to join you
in weeping is what I desire.
Virgin of virgins, chosen,
do not be bitter toward me;
make me weep with you.
Grant that I may bear the death of Christ,
share his passion,
and remember his wounds.
Let me be wounded with his wounds;
let me be inebriated by the Cross
and the blood of your Son.
Lest I be set aflame by the fires of death,
Virgin, may I be defended by you
on the day of judgment.
Christ, when it is time to pass,
grant that through your Mother I may come

fac, ut tecum lúgeam.
Fac ut árdeat cor meum
in amándo Christum Deum
ut sibi compláceam.
Sancta Mater, istud agas
crucifíxi fige plagas
cordi meo válide.
Tui Nati vulneráti,
tam dignáti pro me pati,
poenas mecum dívide.
Fac me tecum pie flere,
crucifíxo condolére,
donec ego víxero.
Iuxta Crucem tecum stare,
et me tibi sociáre
in planctu desídero.
Virgo vírginum, praeclára,
mihi iam non sis amára;
fac me tecum plángere.
Fac ut portem Christi mortem,
passiónis fac consórtem,
et plagas recólere.
Fac me plagis vulnerári;
fac me Cruce inebriári
et cruóre Fílii.
Flammis ne urar succénsus,
per te, Virgo, sim defénsus
in die iudícii.
Christe, cum sit hinc exíre,
da per Matrem me veníre

to the palm of victory.
When my body dies,
give to my soul
the glory of paradise.
Amen.

ad palmam victóriae.
Quando corpus moriétur,
fac ut ánimae donétur
paradísi glória.
Amen.

ITE AD JOSEPH

Vírginum custos et pater, sancte Joseph, cujus fidéli custódiæ ipsa Innocéntia Christus Jesus et Virgo vírginum María commíssa fuit: te per hoc utrúmque caríssimi pignus Jesum et Maríam óbsecro et obtéstor, ut me, ab omni immundítia præservátum, mente incontamináta, puro corde et casto córpore Jesu et Maríæ semper fácias castíssime famulari. Amen

O Blessed Saint Joseph, faithful guardian and protector of virgins, to whom God entrusted Jesus and Mary, I implore you by the love which you did bear them, to preserve me from every defilement of soul and body, that I may always serve Jesus and Mary in holiness and purity of love. Amen.

Favorite Psalms

Note that the Latin Vulgate psalms are numbered differently than Scripture translations in current use. This difference is because the Vulgate inherited its numbering from the Septuagint, the Greek version of the Old Testament, while more recent editions use the system that is employed by the Hebrew Masoretic text. You may also notice that the Latin and English verse numbers do not always correspond to the same text. These were choices made by the respective translators.

PSALM 8

2   O Lord, our Master, how the majesty of thy name fills all the earth! Thy greatness is high above heaven itself.

3   Thou hast made the lips of children, of infants at the breast, vocal with praise, to confound thy enemies; to silence malicious and revengeful tongues.

4   I look up at those heavens of thine, the work of thy hands, at the moon and the stars, which thou hast set in their places;

5   what is man that thou shouldst remember him? What is Adam's breed, that it should claim thy care?

6   Thou hast placed him only a little below the angels, crowning him with glory and honour,

7   and bidding him rule over the works of thy hands.

8   Thou hast put them all under his dominion, the sheep and the cattle, and the wild beasts besides;

9   the birds in the sky, and the fish in the sea, that travel by the sea's paths.

10 O Lord, our Master, how the majesty of thy name fills all the earth!

PSALM 23

1   The Lord is my shepherd; how can I lack anything?

2   He gives me a resting-place where there is green pasture, leads me out to the cool water's brink, refreshed and content.

PSALM 8

2 Dómine, Dóminus noster, quam admirábile est
nomen tuum in univérsa terra! quóniam eleváta est
magnificéntia tua super caelos.

3 Ex ore infántium et lacténtium perfecísti laudem propter
inímicos tuos, ut déstruas inimícum et ultórem.

4 Quóniam vidébo caelos tuos, ópera digitórum tuórum,
lunam et stellas quae tu fundásti.

5 Quid est homo, quod memor es eius? aut fílius hóminis,
quóniam vísitas eum?

6 Minuísti eum paulo minus ab ángelis; glória et honóre
coronásti eum;

7 et constituísti eum super ópera mánuum tuárum.

8 Omnia subiecísti sub pédibus eius, oves et boves
univérsas: ínsuper et pécora campi.

9 Vólucres caeli, et pisces maris, qui perámbulant sémitas
maris.

10 Dómine, Dóminus noster, quam admirábile est nomen
tuum in univérsa terra!

PSALM 22

1 Dóminus regit me, et nihil mihi déerit: in loco páscuae
ibi me collocávit.

2 Super aquam refectiónis educávit me: ánimam meam
convértit.

3 As in honour pledged, by sure paths he leads me;
4 dark be the valley about my path, hurt I fear none while he is with me; thy rod, thy crook are my comfort.
5 Envious my foes watch, while thou dost spread a banquet for me; richly thou dost anoint my head with oil, well filled my cup.
6 All my life thy loving favour pursues me; through the long years the Lord's house shall be my dwelling-place.

PSALM 27

1 The Lord is my light and my deliverance; whom have I to fear? The Lord watches over my life; whom shall I hold in dread?
2 Vainly the malicious close about me, as if they would tear me in pieces, vainly my enemies threaten me; all at once they stumble and fall.
3 Though a whole host were arrayed against me, my heart would be undaunted; though an armed onset should threaten me, still I would not lose my confidence.
4 One request I have ever made of the Lord, let me claim it still, to dwell in the Lord's house my whole life long, resting content in the Lord's goodness, gazing at his temple.
5 In his royal tent he hides me, in the inmost recess of his royal tent, safe from peril.

3   Dedúxit me super sémitas iustítiae, propter nomen suum.

4   Nam, et si ambulávero in médio umbrae mortis, non timébo mala: quóniam tu mecum es. Virga tua, et báculus tuus: ipsa me consoláta sunt.

5   Parásti in conspéctu meo mensam, advérsus eos, qui tríbulant me. Impinguásti in óleo caput meum: et calix meus inébrians quam praeclárus est!

6   Et misericórdia tua subsequétur me ómnibus diébus vitae meae: Et ut inhábitem in domo Dómini, in longitúdinem diérum.

PSALM 26

1   Dóminus illuminátio mea, et salus mea, quem timébo? Dóminus protéctor vitae meae, a quo trepidábo?

2   Dum apprópiant super me nocéntes, ut edant carnes meas: Qui tríbulant me inimíci mei, ipsi infirmáti sunt, et cecidérunt.

3   Si consístant advérsum me castra, non timébit cor meum. Si exsúrgat advérsum me praélium, in hoc ego sperábo.

4   Unam pétii a Dómino, hanc requíram, ut inhábitem in domo Dómini ómnibus diébus vitae meae: Ut vídeam voluptátem Dómini, et vísitem templum eius.

5   Quóniam abscóndit me in tabernáculo suo: in die malórum protéxit me in abscóndito tabernáculi sui.

6   On a rock fastness he lifts me high up; my head rises high above the enemies that encompass me. I will make an offering of triumphant music in this tabernacle of his, singing and praising the Lord.

7   Listen to my voice, Lord, when I cry to thee; hear and spare.

8   True to my heart's promise, I have eyes only for thee; I long, Lord, for thy presence.

9   Do not hide thy face, do not turn away from thy servant in anger, but give me still thy aid; do not forsake me, do not neglect me, O God, my defender.

10   Father and mother may neglect me, but the Lord takes me into his care.

11   Lord, shew me the way thou hast chosen for me, guide me along the sure path, beset as I am with enemies;

12   do not give me over to the will of my oppressors, when false witnesses stand up to accuse me, breathe out threats against me.

13   My faith is, I will yet live to see the Lord's mercies.

14   Wait patiently for the Lord to help thee; be brave, and let thy heart take comfort; wait patiently for the Lord.

Psalm 34

2   At all times I will bless the Lord; his praise shall be on my lips continually.

3   Be all my boasting in the Lord; listen to me, humble souls, and rejoice.

6   In petra exaltávit me: et nunc exaltávit caput meum
    super inimícos meos. Circuívi, et immolávi in
    tabernáculo eius hóstiam vociferatiónis: cantábo, et
    psalmum dicam Dómino.

7   Exaúdi, Dómine, vocem meam, qua clamávi ad te:
    miserére mei, et exaúdi me.

8   Tibi dixit cor meum, exquisívit te fácies mea: fáciem
    tuam, Dómine, requíram.

9   Ne avértas fáciem tuam a me: ne declínes in ira a servo
    tuo. Adiútor meus esto: ne derelínquas me, neque
    despícias me, Deus, salutáris meus.

10 Quóniam pater meus, et mater mea dereliquérunt me:
    Dóminus autem assúmpsit me.

11 Legem pone mihi, Dómine, in via tua: et dírige me in
    sémitam rectam propter inimícos meos.

12 Ne tradíderis me in ánimas tribulántium me: quóniam
    insurrexérunt in me testes iníqui, et mentíta est
    iníquitas sibi.

13 Credo vidére bona Dómini in terra vivéntium.

14 Exspécta Dóminum, viríliter age: et confortétur cor
    tuum, et sústine Dóminum.

PSALM 33

2   Benedícam Dóminum in omni témpore: semper laus
    eius in ore meo.

3   In Dómino laudábitur ánima mea: áudiant mansuéti, et
    laeténtur.

4   Come, sing the Lord's praise with me, let us extol his name together.

5   Did I not look to the Lord, and find a hearing; did he not deliver me from all my terrors?

6   Ever look to him, and in him find happiness; here is no room for downcast looks.

7   Friendless folk may still call upon the Lord and gain his ear, and be rescued from all their afflictions.

8   Guardian of those who fear the Lord, his angel encamps at their side, and brings deliverance.

9   How gracious the Lord is! Taste and prove it; blessed is the man that learns to trust in him.

10 It is for you, his chosen servants, to fear the Lord; those who fear him never go wanting.

11 Justly do the proud fall into hunger and want; blessing they lack not that look to him.

12 Know, then, my children, what the fear of the Lord is; come and listen to my teaching.

13 Long life, and prosperous days, who would have these for the asking?

14 My counsel is, keep thy tongue clear of harm, and thy lips free from every treacherous word.

15 Naught of evil cherish thou, but rather do good; let peace be all thy quest and aim.

16 On the upright the Lord's eye ever looks favourably; his ears are open to their pleading.

17 Perilous is his frown for the wrong-doers; he will soon make their name vanish from the earth.

18 Roused by the cry of the innocent, the Lord sets them free from all their afflictions.

4 Magnificáte Dómin um mecum: et exaltémus nomen eius in idípsum.

5 Exquisívi Dóminum, et exaudívit me: et ex ómnibus tribulatiónibus meis erípuit me.

6 Accédite ad eum, et illuminámini: et fácies vestrae non confundéntur.

7 Iste pauper clamávit, et Dóminus exaudívit eum: et de ómnibus tribulatiónibus eius salvávit eum.

8 Immíttet Ángelus Dómini in circúitu timéntium eum: et erípiet eos.

9 Gustáte, et vidéte quóniam suávis est Dóminus: beátus vir, qui sperat in eo.

10 Timéte Dóminum, omnes sancti eius: quóniam non est inópia timéntibus eum.

11 Dívites eguérunt et esuriérunt: inquiréntes autem Dóminum non minuéntur omni bono.

12 Veníte, fílii, audíte me: timórem Dómini docébo vos.

13 Quis est homo qui vult vitam: díligit dies vidére bonos?

14 Próhibe linguam tuam a malo: et lábia tua ne loquántur dolum.

15 Divérte a malo, et fac bonum: inquíre pacem, et perséquere eam.

16 Óculi Dómini super iustos: et aures eius in preces eórum.

17 Vultus autem Dómini super faciéntes mala: ut perdat de terra memóriam eórum.

18 Clamavérunt iusti, et Dóminus exaudívit eos: et ex ómnibus tribulatiónibus eórum liberávit eos.

19 So near is he to patient hearts, so ready to defend the humbled spirit.

20 Though a hundred trials beset the innocent, the Lord will bring him safely through them all.

21 Under the Lord's keeping, every bone of his is safe; not one of them shall suffer harm

22 Villainy hastes to its own undoing; the enemies of innocence will bear their punishment.

23 The Lord will claim his servant as his own; they go unreproved that put their trust in him.

PSALM 42

2 O God, my whole soul longs for thee, as a deer for running water;

3 my whole soul thirsts for God, the living God; shall I never again make my pilgrimage into God's presence?

4 Morning and evening, my diet still of tears! Daily I must listen to the taunt, Where is thy God now?

5 Memories come back to me yet, melting the heart; how once I would join with the throng, leading the way to God's house, amid cries of joy and thanksgiving, and all the bustle of holiday.

6 Soul, art thou still downcast? Wilt thou never be at peace? Wait for God's help; I will not cease to cry out in thankfulness, My champion and my God.

19 Iuxta est Dóminus iis, qui tribuláto sunt corde: et húmiles spíritu salvábit.

20 Multae tribulatiónes iustórum: et de ómnibus his liberábit eos Dóminus.

21 Custódit Dóminus ómnia ossa eórum: unum ex his non conterétur.

22 Mors peccatórum péssima: et qui odérunt iustum, delínquent.

23 Rédimet Dóminus ánimas servórum suórum: et non delínquent omnes qui sperant in eo.

PSALM 41

2 Quemádmodum desíderat cervus ad fontes aquárum: ita desíderat ánima mea ad te, Deus.

3 Sitívit ánima mea ad Deum fortem vivum: quando véniam, et apparébo ante fáciem Dei?

4 Fuérunt mihi lácrimae meae panes die ac nocte: dum dícitur mihi cotídie: Ubi est Deus tuus?

5 Haec recordátus sum, et effúdi in me ánimam meam: quóniam transíbo in locum tabernáculi admirábilis, usque ad domum Dei. In voce exsultatiónis, et confessiónis: sonus epulántis.

6 Quare tristis es, ánima mea? et quare contúrbas me? Spera in Deo, quóniam adhuc confitébor illi: salutáre vultus mei, et Deus meus.

7   In my sad mood I will think of thee, here in this land of Jordan and Hermon, here on Misar mountain.

8   One depth makes answer to another amid the roar of the floods thou sendest; wave after wave, crest after crest overwhelms me.

9   Would he but lighten the day with his mercy, what praise would I sing at evening to the Lord God who is life for me!

10   Thou art my stronghold, I cry out to him still; hast thou never a thought for me? Must I go mourning, with enemies pressing me hard;

11   racked by the ceaseless taunts of my persecutors, Where is thy God now?

12   Soul, art thou still downcast? Wilt thou never be at peace? Wait for God's help; I will not cease to cry out in thankfulness, My champion and my God.

Psalm 51

3   Have mercy on me, O God, as thou art ever rich in mercy; in the abundance of thy compassion, blot out the record of my misdeeds.

4   Wash me clean, cleaner yet, from my guilt, purge me of my sin,

5   the guilt which I freely acknowledge, the sin which is never lost to my sight.

6   Thee only my sins have offended; it is thy will I have disobeyed; thy sentence was deserved, and still when thou givest award thou hast right on thy side.

7   Ad meípsum ánima mea conturbáta est: proptérea memor ero tui de terra Iordánis, et Hermóniim a monte módico.

8   Abýssus abýssum ínvocat, in voce cataractárum tuárum. Omnia excélsa tua, et fluctus tui super me transiérunt.

9   In die mandávit Dóminus misericórdiam suam: et nocte cánticum eius. Apud me orátio Deo vitae meae, dicam Deo: Suscéptor meus es.

10 Quare oblítus es mei? et quare contristátus incédo, dum afflígit me inimícus?

11 Dum confringúntur ossa mea, exprobravérunt mihi qui tríbulant me inimíci mei. Dum dicunt mihi per síngulos dies: Ubi est Deus tuus? quare tristis es, ánima mea? et quare contúrbas me?

12 Spera in Deo, quóniam adhuc confitébor illi: salutáre vultus mei, et Deus meus.

Psalm 50

3   Miserére mei, Deus, secúndum magnam misericórdiam tuam.Et secúndum multitúdinem miseratiónum tuárum, dele iniquitátem meam.

4   Ámplius lava me ab iniquitáte mea: et a peccáto meo munda me.

5   Quóniam iniquitátem meam ego cognósco: et peccátum meum contra me est semper.

6   Tibi soli peccávi, et malum coram te feci: ut iustificéris in sermónibus tuis, et vincas cum iudicáris.

7   For indeed, I was born in sin; guilt was with me already when my mother conceived me.

8   But thou art a lover of faithfulness, and now, deep in my heart, thy wisdom has instructed me.

9   Sprinkle me with a wand of hyssop, and I shall be clean; washed, I shall be whiter than snow;

10 tidings send me of good news and rejoicing, and the body that lies in the dust shall thrill with pride.

11 Turn thy eyes away from my sins, blot out the record of my guilt;

12 my God, bring a clean heart to birth within me; breathe new life, true life, into my being.

13 Do not banish me from thy presence, do not take thy holy spirit away from me;

14 give me back the comfort of thy saving power, and strengthen me in generous resolve.

15 So will I teach the wicked to follow thy paths; sinners shall come back to thy obedience.

16 My God, my divine Deliverer, save me from the guilt of bloodshed! This tongue shall boast of thy mercies;

17 O Lord, thou wilt open my lips, and my mouth shall tell of thy praise.

18 Thou hast no mind for sacrifice, burnt-offerings, if I brought them, thou wouldst refuse;

19 here, O God, is my sacrifice, a broken spirit; a heart that is humbled and contrite thou, O God, wilt never disdain.

20 Lord, in thy great love send prosperity to Sion, so that the walls of Jerusalem may rise again.

7 Ecce enim, in iniquitátibus concéptus sum: et in peccátis concépit me mater mea.

8 Ecce enim, veritátem dilexísti: incérta et occúlta sapiéntiae tuae manifestásti mihi.

9 Aspérges me hyssópo, et mundábor: lavábis me, et super nivem dealbábor.

10 Audítui meo dabis gáudium et laetítiam: et exsultábunt ossa humiliáta.

11 Avérte fáciem tuam a peccátis meis: et omnes iniquitátes meas dele.

12 Cor mundum crea in me, Deus: et spíritum rectum ínnova in viscéribus meis.

13 Ne proícias me a fácie tua: et spíritum sanctum tuum ne aúferas a me.

14 Redde mihi laetítiam salutáris tui: et spíritu principáli confírma me.

15 Docébo iníquos vias tuas: et ímpii ad te converténtur.

16 Líbera me de sanguínibus, Deus, Deus salútis meae: et exsultábit lingua mea iustítiam tuam.

17 Dómine, lábia mea apéries: et os meum annuntiábit laudem tuam.

18 Quóniam si voluísses sacrifícium, dedíssem útique: holocaústis non delectáberis.

19 Sacrifícium Deo spíritus contribulátus: cor contrítum, et humiliátum, Deus, non despícies.

20 Benígne fac, Dómine, in bona voluntáte tua Sion: ut aedificéntur muri Ierúsalem.

21 Then indeed thou wilt take pleasure in solemn sacrifice, in gift and burnt-offering; then indeed bullocks will be laid upon thy altar.

PSALM 91

1 Content if thou be to live with the most High for thy defence, under his Almighty shadow abiding still,

2 him thy refuge, him thy stronghold thou mayst call, thy own God, in whom is all thy trust.

3 He it is will rescue thee from every treacherous lure, every destroying plague. 4 His wings for refuge, nestle thou shalt under his care,

5 his faithfulness thy watch and ward. Nothing shalt thou have to fear from nightly terrors,

6 from the arrow that flies by day-light, from pestilence that walks to and fro in the darkness, from the death that wastes under the noon.

7 Though a thousand fall at thy side, ten thousand at thy right hand, it shall never come next or near thee;

8 rather, thy eyes shall look about thee, and see the reward of sinners.

9 He, the Lord, is thy refuge; thou hast found a stronghold in the most High.

10 There is no harm that can befall thee, no plague that shall come near thy dwelling.

11 He has given charge to his angels concerning thee, to watch over thee wheresoever thou goest;

21 Tunc acceptábis sacrifícium iustítiae, oblatiónes, et holocaústa: tunc impónent super altáre tuum vítulos.

Psalm 90

1 Qui hábitat in adiutório Altíssimi, in protectióne Dei caeli commorábitur.

2 Dicet Dómino: Suscéptor meus es tu, et refúgium meum: Deus meus sperábo in eum.

3 Quóniam ipse liberávit me de láqueo venántium, et a verbo áspero.

4 Scápulis suis obumbrábit tibi: et sub pennis eius sperábis.

5 Scuto circúmdabit te véritas eius: non timébis a timóre noctúrno,

6 A sagítta volánte in die, a negótio perambulánte in ténebris: ab incúrsu, et daemónio meridiáno.

7 Cadent a látere tuo mille, et decem míllia a dextris tuis: ad te autem non appropinquábit.

8 Verúmtamen óculis tuis considerábis: et retributiónem peccatórum vidébis.

9 Quóniam tu es, Dómine, spes mea: Altíssimum posuísti refúgium tuum.

10 Non accédet ad te malum: et flagéllum non appropinquábit tabernáculo tuo.

11 Quóniam Ángelis suis mandávit de te: ut custódiant te in ómnibus viis tuis.

12 they will hold thee up with their hands lest thou shouldst chance to trip on a stone.

13 Thou shalt tread safely on asp and adder, crush lion and serpent under thy feet.

14 He trusts in me, mine it is to rescue him; he acknowledges my name, from me he shall have protection;

15 when he calls upon me, I will listen, in affliction I am at his side, to bring him safety and honour.

16 Length of days he shall have to content him, and find in me deliverance.

Psalm 95

1 Come, friends, rejoice we in the Lord's honour; cry we out merrily to God, our strength and deliverer;

2 with praises court his presence, singing a joyful psalm!

3 A high God is the Lord, a king high above all the gods;

4 beneath his hand lie the depths of earth, his are the mountain peaks;

5 his the ocean, for who but he created it? What other power fashioned the dry land?

6 Come in, then, fall we down in worship, bowing the knee before God who made us.

7 Who but the Lord is our God? And what are we, but folk of his pasturing, sheep that follow his beckoning hand?

8 Would you but listen to his voice to-day! Do not harden your hearts,

12 In mánibus portábunt te: ne forte offéndas ad lápidem pedem tuum.

13 Super áspidem, et basilíscum ambulábis: et conculcábis leónem et dracónem.

14 Quóniam in me sperávit, liberábo eum: prótegam eum, quóniam cognóvit nomen meum.

15 Clamábit ad me, et ego exaúdiam eum: cum ipso sum in tribulatióne: erípiam eum et glorificábo eum.

16 Longitúdine diérum replébo eum: et osténdam illi salutáre meum.

PSALM 94

1 Veníte, exsultémus Dómino: iubilémus Deo salutári nostro:

2 Praeoccupémus fáciem eius in confessióne: et in psalmis iubilémus ei.

3 Quóniam Deus magnus Dóminus: et Rex magnus super omnes deos.

4 Quia in manu eius sunt omnes fines terrae: et altitúdines   móntium ipsíus sunt.

5 Quóniam ipsíus est mare, et ipse fecit illud: et siccam manus eius formavérunt.

6 Veníte, adorémus, et procidámus, et plorémus ante Dóminum qui fecit nos.

7 Quia ipse est Dóminus Deus noster, et nos pópulus páscuae eius, et oves manus eius.

8 Hódie si vocem eius audiéritis, nolíte obduráre corda vestra:

9   as they were hardened once at Meriba, at Massa in the wilderness. Your fathers put me to the test, challenged me, as if they lacked proof of my power,

10   for forty years together; from that generation I turned away in loathing; These, I said, are ever wayward hearts,

11   these have never learned to obey me. And I took an oath in anger, They shall never attain my rest.

PSALM 103

1   Bless the Lord, my soul, unite, all my powers, to bless that holy name.

2   Bless the Lord, my soul, remembering all he has done for thee,

3   how he pardons all thy sins, heals all thy mortal ills,

4   rescues thy life from deadly peril, crowns thee with the blessings of his mercy;

5   how he contents all thy desire for good, restores thy youth, as the eagle's plumage is restored.

6   The Lord's acts are acts of justice, every wronged soul he offers redress.

7   The Lord, who told Moses his secrets, who shewed the sons of Israel his power!

8   How pitying and gracious the Lord is, how patient, how rich in mercy!

9   He will not always be finding fault, his frown does not last for ever;

9   Sicut in irritatióne secúndum diem tentatiónis in desérto: ubi tentavérunt me patres vestri, probavérunt me, et vidérunt ópera mea.

10   Quadragínta annis offénsus fui generatióni illi, et dixi: Semper hi errant corde.

11   Et isti non cognovérunt vias meas, ut iurávi in ira mea: Si introíbunt in réquiem meam.

Psalm 102

1   Bénedic, ánima mea, Dómino: et ómnia, quae intra me sunt, nómini sancto eius.

2   Bénedic, ánima mea, Dómino: et noli oblivísci omnes retributiónes eius.

3   Qui propitiátur ómnibus iniquitátibus tuis: qui sanat omnes infirmitátes tuas.

4   Qui rédimit de intéritu vitam tuam: qui corónat te in misericórdia et miseratiónibus.

5   Qui replet in bonis desidérium tuum: renovábitur ut áquilae iuvéntus tua:

6   Fáciens misericórdias Dóminus: et iudícium ómnibus iniúriam patiéntibus.

7   Notas fecit vias suas Móysi, fíliis Israël voluntátes suas.

8   Miserátor, et miséricors Dóminus: longánimis, et multum miséricors.

9   Non in perpétuum irascétur: neque in aetérnum comminábitur.

10 he does not treat us as our sins deserve, does not exact the penalty of our wrong-doing.

11 High as heaven above the earth towers his mercy for the men that fear him;

12 far as the east is from the west, he clears away our guilt from us.

13 For his own worshippers, the Lord has a father's pity;

14 does he not know the stuff of which we are made, can he forget that we are only dust?

15 Man's life is like the grass, he blooms and dies like a flower in the fields;

16 once the hot wind has passed over, it has gone, forgotten by the place where it grew.

17 But the Lord's worshippers know no beginning or end of his mercy; he will keep faith with their children's children,

18 do they but hold fast by his covenant, and live mindful of his law.

19 The Lord has set up his throne in heaven, rules with universal sway.

20 Bless the Lord, all you angels of his; angels of sovereign strength, that carry out his commandment, attentive to the word he utters;

21 bless the Lord, all you hosts of his, the servants that perform his will;

22 bless the Lord, all you creatures of his, in every corner of his dominion; and thou, my soul, bless the Lord.

10 Non secúndum peccáta nostra fecit nobis: neque secúndum iniquitátes nostras retríbuit nobis.

11 Quóniam secúndum altitúdinem caeli a terra: corroborávit misericórdiam suam super timéntes se.

12 Quantum distat ortus ab occidénte: longe fecit a nobis iniquitátes nostras.

13 Quómodo miserétur pater filiórum, misértus est Dóminus timéntibus se:

14 quóniam ipse cognóvit figméntum nostrum; recordátus est quóniam pulvis sumus.

15 Homo, sicut foenum dies eius; tamquam flos agri sic efflorébit:

16 quóniam spíritus pertransíbit in illo, et non subsístet: et non cognóscet ámplius locum suum.

17 Misericórdia autem Dómini ab aetérno, et usque in aetérnum super timéntes eum. Et iustítia illíus in fílios filiórum, his qui servant testaméntum eius:

18 Et mémores sunt mandatórum ipsíus, ad faciéndum ea.

19 Dóminus in caelo parávit sedem suam: et regnum ipsíus ómnibus dominábitur.

20 Benedícite Dómino, omnes Ángeli eius: poténtes virtúte, faciéntes verbum illíus, ad audiéndam vocem sermónum eius.

21 Benedícite Dómino, omnes virtútes eius: minístri eius, qui fácitis voluntátem eius.

22 Benedícite Dómino, ómnia ópera eius: in omni loco dominatiónis eius, bénedic, ánima mea, Dómino.

PSALM 121

1 I lift up my eyes to the hills, to find deliverance;
2 from the Lord deliverance comes to me, the Lord who made heaven and earth.
3 Never will he who guards thee allow thy foot to stumble; never fall asleep at his post!
4 Such a guardian has Israel, one who is never weary, never sleeps;
5 it is the Lord that guards thee, the Lord that stands at thy right hand to give thee shelter.
6 The sun's rays by day, the moon's by night, shall have no power to hurt thee.
7 The Lord will guard thee from all evil; the Lord will protect thee in danger;
8 the Lord will protect thy journeying and thy home-coming, henceforth and for ever.

PSALM 130

1 Out of the depths I cry to thee, O Lord;
2 Master, listen to my voice; let but thy ears be attentive to the voice that calls on thee for pardon.
3 If thou, Lord, wilt keep record of our iniquities, Master, who has strength to bear it?
4 Ah, but with thee there is forgiveness; be thy name ever revered.

PSALM 120

1   Leávi óculos meos in montes, unde véniet auxílium mihi.

2   Auxílium meum a Dómino, qui fecit caelum et terram.

3   Non det in commotiónem pedem tuum: neque dormítet qui custódit te.

4   Ecce, non dormitábit neque dórmiet, qui custódit Israël.

5   Dóminus custódit te, Dóminus protéctio tua, super manum déxteram tuam.

6   Per diem sol non uret te: neque luna per noctem.

7   Dóminus custódit te ab omni malo: custódiat ánimam tuam Dóminus.

8   Dóminus custódiat intróitum tuum, et éxitum tuum: ex hoc nunc, et usque in saéculum.

PSALM 129

1   De profúndis clamávi ad te, Dómine: Dómine, exáudi vocem meam:

2   Fiant aures tuae intendéntes, in vocem deprecatiónis meae.

3   Si iniquitátes observáveris, Dómine: Dómine, quis sustinébit?

4   Quia apud te propitiátio est: et propter legem tuam sustínui te, Dómine.

5   I wait for the Lord, for his word of promise my soul waits;
6   patient my soul waits, as ever watchman that looked for the day. Patient as watchman at dawn,
7   for the Lord Israel waits, the Lord with whom there is mercy, with whom is abundant power to ransom.
8   He it is that will ransom Israel from all his iniquities.

Psalm 139

1   Lord, I lie open to thy scrutiny; thou knowest me,
2   knowest when sit down and when I rise up again, canst read my thoughts from far away.
3   Walk I or sleep I, thou canst tell; no movement of mine but thou art watching it.
4   Before ever the words are framed on my lips, all my thought is known to thee;
5   rearguard and vanguard, thou dost compass me about, thy hand still laid upon me.
6   Such wisdom as thine is far beyond my reach, no thought of mine can attain it.
7   Where can I go, then, to take refuge from thy spirit, to hide from thy view?
8   If I should climb up to heaven, thou art there; if I sink down to the world beneath, thou art present still.
9   If I could wing my way eastwards, or find a dwelling beyond the western sea,

5   Sustínuit ánima mea in verbo eius: sperávit ánima mea in Dómino.

6   A custódia matutína usque ad noctem: speret Israël in Dómino.

7   Quia apud Dóminum misericórdia: et copiósa apud eum redémptio.

8   Et ipse rédimet Israël, ex ómnibus iniquitátibus eius.

PSALM 138

1   Dómine, probásti me, et cognovísti me:

2   tu cognovísti sessiónem meam, et resurrectiónem meam.

3   Intellexísti cogitatiónes meas de longe: sémitam meam, et funículum meum investigásti.

4   Et omnes vias meas praevidísti: quia non est sermo in lingua mea.

5   Ecce, Dómine, tu cognovísti ómnia novíssima, et antíqua: tu formásti me, et posuísti super me manum tuam.

6   Mirábilis facta est sciéntia tua ex me: confortáta est, et non pótero ad eam.

7   Quo ibo a spíritu tuo? et quo a fácie tua fúgiam?

8   Si ascéndero in caelum, tu illic es: si descéndero in inférnum, ades.

9   Si súmpsero pennas meas dilúculo, et habitávero in extrémis maris:

10 still would I find thee beckoning to me, thy right hand upholding me.

11 Or perhaps I would think to bury myself in darkness; night should surround me, friendlier than day;

12 but no, darkness is no hiding-place from thee, with thee the night shines clear as day itself; light and dark are one.

13 Author, thou, of my inmost being, didst thou not form me in my mother's womb?

14 I praise thee for my wondrous fashioning, for all the wonders of thy creation. Of my soul thou hast full knowledge,

15 and this mortal frame had no mysteries for thee, who didst contrive it in secret, devise its pattern, there in the dark recesses of the earth.

16 All my acts thy eyes have seen, all are set down already in thy record; my days were numbered before ever they came to be.

17 A riddle, O my God, thy dealings with me, so vast their scope!

18 As well count the sand, as try to fathom them; and, were that skill mine, thy own being still confronts me.

19 O God, wouldst thou but make an end of the wicked! Murderers, keep your distance from me!

20 Treacherously they rebel against thee, faithlessly set thee at defiance.

21 Lord, do I not hate the men who hate thee, am I not sick at heart over their rebellion?

22 Surpassing hatred I bear them, count them my sworn enemies.

10 Étenim illuc manus tua dedúcet me: et tenébit me déxtera tua.

11 Et dixi: Fórsitan ténebrae conculcábunt me: et nox illuminátio mea in delíciis meis.

12 Quia ténebrae non obscurabúntur a te, et nox sicut dies illuminábitur: sicut ténebrae eius, ita et lumen eius.

13 Quia tu possedísti renes meos: suscepísti me de útero matris meae.

14 Confitébor tibi quia terribíliter magnificátus es: mirabília ópera tua, et ánima mea cognóscit nimis.

15 Non est occultátum os meum a te, quod fecísti in occúlto: et substántia mea in inferióribus terrae.

16 Imperféctum meum vidérunt óculi tui, et in libro tuo omnes scribéntur: dies formabúntur, et nemo in eis.

17 Mihi autem nimis honorificáti sunt amíci tui, Deus: nimis confortátus est principátus eórum.

18 Dinumerábo eos, et super arénam multiplicabúntur: exsurréxi, et adhuc sum tecum.

19 Si occíderis, Deus, peccatóres: viri sánguinum, declináte a me:

20 Quia dícitis in cogitatióne: Accípient in vanitáte civitátes tuas.

21 Nonne qui odérunt te, Dómine, óderam? et super inimícos tuos tabescébam?

22 Perfécto ódio óderam illos: et inimíci facti sunt mihi.

23 Scrutinize me, O God, as thou wilt, and read my heart;
    put me to the test, and examine my restless thoughts.

24 See if on any false paths my heart is set, and thyself lead
    me in the ways of old.

Psalm 144

1   Blessed be the Lord, my refuge, who makes these hands
    strong for battle, these fingers skilled in fight;

2   the Lord who pities me and grants me safety, who shel-
    ters me and sets me at liberty, who protects me and gives
    me confidence, bowing down nations to my will.

3   Lord, what is Adam's race, that thou givest heed to it,
    what is man, that thou carest for him?

4   Like the wind he goes, like a shadow his days pass.

5   Bid heaven stoop, Lord, and come down to earth; at thy
    touch, the mountains will be wreathed in smoke

6   Brandish thy lightnings, to rout my enemies; shoot thy
    arrows, and throw them into confusion!

7   With heavenly aid, from yonder flood deliver me; rescue
    me from the power of alien foes,

8   who make treacherous promises, and lift their hands in
    perjury.

9   Then, O my God, I will sing thee a new song, on a ten-
    stringed harp I will sound thy praise;

10 the God to whom kings must look for victory, the God
    who has brought his servant David rescue.

23 Proba me, Deus, et scito cor meum: intérroga me, et cognósce sémitas meas.

24 Et vide, si via iniquitátis in me est: et deduc me in via aetérna.

PSALM 143

1 Benedíctus Dóminus, Deus meus, qui docet manus meas ad praélium, et dígitos meos ad bellum.

2 Misericórdia mea, et refúgium meum: suscéptor meus, et liberátor meus: Protéctor meus, et in ipso sperávi: qui subdit pópulum meum sub me.

3 Dómine, quid est homo, quia innotuísti ei? aut fílius hóminis, quia réputas eum?

4 Homo vanitáti símilis factus est: dies eius sicut umbra praetéreunt.

5 Dómine, inclína caelos tuos, et descénde: tange montes, et fumigábunt.

6 Fúlgura coruscatiónem, et dissipábis eos: emítte sagíttas tuas, et conturbábis eos.

7 Emítte manum tuam de alto, éripe me, et líbera me de aquis multis: de manu filiórum alienórum.

8 Quorum os locútum est vanitátem: et déxtera eórum, déxtera iniquitátis.

9 Deus, cánticum novum cantábo tibi: in psaltério decachórdo psallam tibi.

10 Qui das salútem régibus: qui redemísti David, servum tuum, de gládio malígno: éripe me.

11 Save me from the cruel sword, deliver me from the power of alien foes, who make treacherous promises, and lift their hands in perjury.

12 So may our sons grow to manhood, tall as the saplings, our daughters shapely as some column at the turn of a building, it may be, the temple itself.

13 Our garners full, well stored with every kind of plenty, our sheep bearing a thousand-fold, thronging the pasture in their tens of thousands,

14 our oxen straining at the load; no ruined walls, no exile, no lamenting in our streets.

15 Happy men call such a people as this; and is not the people happy, that has the Lord for its God?

Psalm 146

2 Praise the Lord, my soul; while life lasts, I will praise the Lord; of him, my God, shall my songs be while I am here to sing them. Do not put your trust in princes;

3 they are but men, they have no power to save.

4 As soon as the breath leaves his body, man goes back to the dust he belongs to; with that, all his designs will come to nothing.

5 Happier the man who turns to the God of Jacob for help, puts no confidence but in the Lord his God,

6 maker of heaven and earth and sea and all they contain;

11 Et érue me de manu filiórum alienórum, quorum
os locútum est vanitátem: et déxtera eórum, déxtera
iniquitátis:

12 Quorum fílii, sicut novéllae plantatiónes in iuventúte
sua. Fíliae eórum compósitae: circumornátae ut
similitúdo templi.

13 Promptuária eórum plena, eructántia ex hoc in illud.
Oves eórum foetósae, abundántes in egréssibus suis:
boves eórum crassae.

14 Non est ruína macériae, neque tránsitus: neque clamor
in platéis eórum.

15 Beátum dixérunt pópulum, cui haec sunt: beátus
pópulus, cuius Dóminus Deus eius.

PSALM 145

2 Lauda, ánima mea, Dóminum, laudábo Dóminum in
vita mea: psallam Deo meo quámdiu fúero.

3 Nolíte confídere in princípibus: in fíliis hóminum, in
quibus non est salus.

4 Exíbit spíritus eius, et revertétur in terram suam: in illa
die períbunt omnes cogitatiónes eórum.

5 Beátus, cuius Deus Iacob adiútor eius, spes eius in
Dómino, Deo ipsíus:

6 qui fecit caelum et terram, mare, et ómnia, quae in eis
sunt.

7   the God who keeps faith for ever, who redresses wrong, and gives food to the hungry. The Lord, who brings release to the prisoner,

8   the Lord, who gives sight to the blind, the Lord, who comforts the burdened, the Lord, who befriends the innocent!

9   The Lord, who protects the stranger, who defends orphan and widow, who overturns the counsel of the wicked!

10   The Lord, reigning for ever, thy God, Sion, reigning from age to age! Alleluia.

7   Qui custódit veritátem in saéculum, facit iudícium
     iniúriam patiéntibus: dat escam esuriéntibus. Dóminus
     solvit compedítos: Dóminus illúminat caecos.
8   Dóminus érigit elísos, Dóminus díligit iustos.
9   Dóminus custódit ádvenas, pupíllum et víduam suscípiet:
     et vias peccatórum dispérdet.
10   Regnábit Dóminus in saécula, Deus tuus, Sion, in
     generatiónem et generatiónem.

ALPHABETICAL INDEX
OF PRAYERS

AVE

AVE MARIA PRESS

Founded in 1865, Ave Maria Press,
a ministry of the Congregation of
Holy Cross, is a Catholic publishing
company that serves the spiritual and
formative needs of the Church and its
schools, institutions, and ministers;
Christian individuals and families; and
others seeking spiritual nourishment.

For a complete listing of titles from

Ave Maria Press

Sorin Books

Forest of Peace

Christian Classics

visit www.avemariapress.com

AVE MARIA PRESS
Notre Dame, IN
A Ministry of the United States Province of Holy Cross